D0779569

What others are saying about this ...

"Packed full of information, juxtaposed with kind words and wisdom from a woman who has spent her life nurturing filmmakers."
—Barbara Trent, academy award winner,
The Panama Deception

"This book is the most intelligent, insightful and comprehensive guide to finding the money that I have ever read. Carole Dean is the independent filmmaker's best friend!"
—Christopher Ward, award winning
independent filmmaker

"Carole Dean has years of experience both as a producer and a funder, and her new book is full of nuts-and-bolts information from both sides of the fence, told in a conversational and heart-felt manner. Of special interest to filmmakers will be the in-dept interviews with experts in the field, and an extensive appendix chock full of references. A great new addition to the filmmaker's lexicon."
—Morrie Warshawski, Consultant, and Author of
Shaking the Money Tree

" . . . Carole is your mentor throughout the book. She leads wary filmmakers through the dark, daunting forest of 'no's' to the greenlight power of 'yes.' 'No does not mean no,' is her mantra. The sensitive artist as successful producer is a rare commodity. That's about to change. There are myriad, alternative ways to finance a film, without selling your soul, and Carole Lee Dean knows them all."
—Judi Jordan, Editor at Large, *Latin Style Magazine*

"In The Art of Funding Your Film, Carole Dean has assembled insights and wisdom that will prove immensely useful to filmmakers in their search for funding."
—Mark Litwak, Attorney and author

"Carole Dean is well known in the motion picture industry for her innovations and creative genius. In her book, In The Art of Funding Your Film, she has created a superb bible that will serve the novice as well as the seasoned filmmaker. Carole has utilized her experience in the industry and her talent to create a masterpiece - a concise roadmap for financing a film which reads like a novel. This book is a major contribution and is bound to be the catalyst for valuable film production that the Public and scholars would otherwise miss."
—S. G. Fassoulis, film producer

"This book is a good start toward seeing the world of funding through the eyes of experienced funders like Carole Dean and her colleagues. We need to master the techniques outlined here so we can create not just one or two films, but an ongoing body of work which will bring years of provocative insights to the public."

—Patric Hedlund, author and filmmaker

"My hat's off to Carole Dean for writing The Art of Funding Your Film. Written with a spiritual perspective and trust for your intuition, she not only acknowledges these creative forces, but rightfully honors the business process as an art in itself! What a joyful journey into filmmaking."

—Wendy De Rycke, Indie Producer

"Carole Dean's book successfully bridges the gap between the vision of the project and the realities of the market for the serious filmmaker."

—Louise Levison, author of
*Filmmakers and Financing: Business Plans
for Independents*

"Carole Dean's engaging book is as inspiring as *The little Engine that Could.* Even if you feel that maybe it is time to throw in the towel or hang up the saddle after so many battles, Carole and her book provide the informed support needed to go beyond what we may have felt was possible."

—Cinda Jackson, director, producer, and actress

All the great stuff in this book clearly comes from Carole's years in the U.S. film business, but it's hugely appropriate that she came to New Zealand to actually write it. It's a country with a long history of small independent filmmakers creating magic on tiny budgets, and not taking "no" for an answer. That's the road Kiwi Peter Jackson traveled to realize his dream with *Lord of the Rings.* Carole's book will give independents world-wide the courage and inspiration to realize theirs."

—Paul Davidson, Documentary filmmaker,
Marlborough, New Zealand

THE ART OF FUNDING YOUR FILM:

Alternative Financing Concepts

By Carole Lee Dean

To Alton James,

Thank you for your eternal support of the arts.

Carole Dean

Dean Publishing
2003
From the Heart Productions
1455 Mandalay Beach Road
Oxnard, California 93035-2845
www.fromtheheartproductions.com

Cover graphics, JanEva Hornbaker, Mark Larick and
Lisa Liddy, printedpage@cox.net

Camera equipment for cover supplied by *Otto Nemenz*, a founding
donor to the Roy W. Dean grant program, maintaining their eternal
commitment to aid filmmakers.

Model, Juan Lopez

Back Cover slide
Production slide by Juan Lopez and Mark Larick,
Front Cover slides
Faun Kime, producer of *The Tomato Effect,*
Mindy Pomper's film *Save A Man to Fight*
Image from *Hopilavayi,* Producer, Bart Hawkins,
Image of Arn Chorn Pond from *The Flute Player,*produced by Jocelyn
Glatzer & Christine Courtney.
www.thefluteplayer.net
Production Still by Sonith Heng

Table of Contents

Preface, by Patric Hedlund 9

Introduction 15

Chapter 1 Commit or be Committed 21

A Conversation With.Filmmaker Xackery Irving .. 32

Chapter 2 The Perfect Pitch 43

Chapter 3 The Proposal 47

*A Conversation With Writer/Filmmaker
JanEva Hornbaker* 51

Chapter 4 Loading the Bases 63

Chapter 5 Foundations and Grants 67

Chapter 6 Raising Funds From Individuals
and Businesses 79

Chapter 7 Cowboy Economics and
Entrepreneurs By Patric Hedlund 93

*A Conversation With Entertainment Attorney
Mark Litwak* 105

Chapter 8 Financing Independent Films
By Mark Litwak 115

Chapter 9 Alternative Financing: Projects
With Nontraditional Partners 129

Chapter 10 Product Placement and Branding 139

A Conversation With Patricia Ganguzza 145

Chapter 11 Public Television 167

Chapter 12 Guidelines for Change 181

    A Conversation With Morrie Warshawski 181

Chapter 13 Sponsorship is Dead
By Daniel Sherrett...193

Appendix 203

    A "Production Resources for Public Television". 204

    B "Internet Search Tools" 207

    C "Databases, Resources & Tools"....................208

    D "Online Articles"...212

    E "Print Resources" 213

    F "Writing Resources"...215

    G "Business Promotion/Public Relations" 216

    H "Organizations"...217

    I "Funders" 219

    "Top Corporations with a Heart
        for Independent Filmakers"...........................249

    Footnotes...257

Carole Lee Dean, entrepreneur, filmmaker, writer, philanthropist, international speaker, and nutrition advocate.

Thirty years ago Carole Dean took a $20 bill and turned it into a $50 million a year industry when she reinvented the tape and short-end industry in Hollywood. As the president and CEO of From the Heart Productions, Carole has produced over 100 television programs, including the popular cable program, HealthStyles, where she interviewed some of the biggest names in the industry including, Dr. Deepak Chopra, Dr. Weil, and Dr. Caroline Myss.

In 1992 Carole created the Roy W. Dean Grant Foundation in honor of her late father. Today Carole's grant and mentorship programs have provided filmmakers with millions of dollars in goods and services and have played an instrumental role in establishing the careers of some of the industry's most promising filmmakers.

A sought-after international speaker, Carole is currently touring the U.S. with her popular Art of Funding Your Films Workshops. For more information on Carole Dean, or to book her for a workshop in your city please contact Carole's publicist, Tory Jay Berger at tory@spiritualpr.com. Carole has dedicated her life to helping filmmakers and the purchase of this book directly supports documentary and independent filmmakers, we thank you for your support.

www.fromtheheartproductions.com

This book is dedicated to
All the wonderful women in my life
Who have loved me; hated me
Pushed me; pulled me
And supported me
Through thick and thin.

PREFACE

Filmmakers like you and I spend the most challenging hours of our lives in quest of funding and distribution. I welcomed an invitation recently from *RealScreen Magazine* to come to the Yale Club in New York City to give the keynote address for a conference on the worldwide crisis in funding documentary films. New York in autumn is a sparkling delight, energized by crisp winds and merry sunshine, a good place to make new friends and share insights. The prospect of speaking alongside people like Carole Dean made the invitation even more alluring. The Roy W. Dean Film Grant—Carole's method of creating alliances between businesses and emerging filmmakers—has been a catalyst for turning creative visions into real films for many years now. Our forum became a two-day summit conference where some of the world's most knowledgeable and talented independent producers and their funders gathered to tackle the issues we all face.

The euphoria was punctured for a moment by a stern dress-code memo from tradition-bound Yale Club administrators. It stated: "those wearing denim will be escorted from the premises"—an astonishing prohibition for a meeting of Indie filmmakers who live in blue jeans. I joked in my keynote speech (Love, War, and the Joy of Seeking Production Financing) that if Documentary Nation had a flag it would be made of denim. We love our jeans because they are durable, resilient, tough and honest. In fact, independent filmmakers survive in challenging times because we, too, are durable, resilient, tough and honest—and so is the best of our work.

These are challenging times. The art of funding independent films is a rapidly transforming terrain. There is a virtual economic blockade in American film and most electronic media against vibrant public debate on complex issues. Changes in the FCC regulatory environment, in production and distribution technologies, and in rapid ownership consolidation have changed contract practices and market dynamics. Yet there has never been a time when the world was more in need of energetic discussion of independent ideas.

European countries, Canada and Australia provide economic subsidies to encourage independent film culture because it brings a rich mix of new visions into public dialogue. They know that maintaining the health of independent voices is like supporting biodiversity, adding to the gene pool of ideas to help solve the challenges of our times. Homo Sapiens are a story-telling species. Culture is our most profound technology, but evolution is always a struggle.

Here in the U.S., indies must become entrepreneurial. Developing sustainable business models matters. Learning how to pay yourself is both practical and patriotic. This book is a good start toward seeing the world of funding through the eyes of experienced funders like Carole Dean and her colleagues. We need to master the techniques outlined here so we can create not just one or two films, but an ongoing body of work which will bring years of provocative insights to the public.

Somewhere, back in the 20th century, a myth arose that independent filmmakers are unrealistic and impractical. In fact, you have opened this book today because you are a practical person determined to find a way to navigate intelligently through a popular culture, government policies and an economic system that are too often driven by fantasy, fictions, spin and denial. In such a society, independents who look at events with a fresh lense are often the realists. But being sane in an asylum is no consolation. Your good-natured revenge is to put the ideas in this book to work fruitfully. Get funded. Be successful. Make many films.

I am delighted that Carole flew off to her hideaway in New Zealand shortly after our New York meeting to capture within these pages the spirit of adventure and opportunity of that event. We owe her our gratitude for making it possible to curl up in comfortable jeans at home with a cat in our lap to explore these strategies—with absolutely no fear of being escorted from the premises. Please read this book carefully, and put the good news here to work. Carole has combined a rare sense of fun with practical information to both raise your spirits and guide your steps on the journey to launch your film successfully. Enjoy, and remember to send us an invitation to the premiers.

—Patric Hedlund
5/05/03, Pine Mountain, CA
Author of *A Bread Crumb Trail Through the PBS Jungle:*
The Independent Producer's Survival Guide
(http://www.forests.com/breadcrumb)

ACKNOWLEDGEMENTS

Tory Berger is the person who said "Go to New Zealand and write a book for filmmakers." Thank you Tory for your constant support.

When I talked to my Aunt Beth and my uncle Grady they said, "After all these years in the business, you know more than you think you do, write that book!"

My friend of 30 years, Branwen Edwards, became my life coach and she pulled one chapter after another out of me, always supporting and encouraging me.

Janeva Hornbaker took over as "the editor from heaven." Using her library and research background, she made sure we were accurate and added her many writing talents and Sagittarian humor to this book.

Dr. Vijay P. Kumar and Dr. Victor B. Lawrence are to be thanked for their support of *From the Heart*.

The chapters by Patric Hedlund, Morrie Warshawski, Patricia Ganguzza, Mark Litwak, Xackery Irving and Dan Sherrett are all gifts for your guidance in funding your films. You could not have better mentors.

There are many important stories in here about other filmmakers and things they learned while "in the trenches," and we greatly appreciate their kindness in sharing these experiences.

The cover graphic was shot by Mark Larick as a gift. Isn't this a great industry to have talented people donate their time to support our grants?

To the many people who helped me that are not mentioned, please know that this was a cooperative labor of love and I thank you for your generous support.

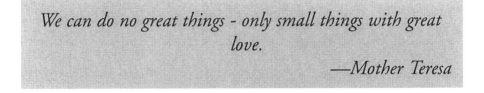

We can do no great things - only small things with great love.

—*Mother Teresa*

INTRODUCTION

You are a filmmaker because you are an artist and a visionary. Where else are you going to find a job that encourages you to create something based on your ideas and thoughts, then get to see it all dance across a 25-foot screen? What other career gives you the opportunity to design something that has the potential to inspire so many people? Filmmaking is a passion that infuses every fiber of your being. It challenges you to reach beyond your potential and allows you to observe the World from a unique perspective.

Film production is also one of the most demanding careers you could choose. During the course of your career you will be required to make an endless number of artistic decisions that will ultimately affect the final outcome your film. Each stage of production is paved with potential pitfalls. If you screw something up in production, you'll pay dearly for it in post. Of course the upside to the frenetic pace of your chosen career is that you will never be bored. Filmmakers seem to thrive on all the twists and turns that come with the job, and they love to talk about their latest war stories.

Just grab a toffee-nut latte and a table at Starbucks over on Hollywood Boulevard and you will hear it all, from passionate debates over the best format and the latest editing equipment, to a broad range of esoteric criticism on some rogue director's bizarre shooting style. What you probably won't hear is the excited banter of filmmakers discussing the latest in funding.

There is more to filmmaking than stepping behind a camera. A film's life does not begin with production and end with postproduction.

There is another stage that is equally important. I'll give you a few hints: decisions made during this stage will determine the very essence of your film, including where it will go, who will see it, what it will say, and whether or not it will survive. It is a stage that occurs long before you dust off your camera, and it requires just as much artistic skill as directing and editing.

You were probably going take a wild stab based on the title of this book and guess preproduction funding, only the part about it requiring as much artistic skill as directing and editing threw you, right?

Always go with your first answer. Preproduction funding is the most critical stage of your film's life. If you don't learn the latest funding techniques and marketing trends you will not survive in this industry. Your future career as a filmmaker and the integrity of your film are both on the line. Do you still want to set this book down and get right to the art of directing?

If you do you're not unlike the majority of those filmmakers over at Starbucks. By the way, have you ever wondered why there are so many filmmakers sitting around drinking coffee in the middle of the day when they could be out there making movies? Maybe it's because they don't happen to have a couple hundred thousand dollars lying around to support their film habit.

If you don't have funding you don't have a film. You might be able to pull off a small project with the help of your little plastic buddies, *Visa* and *MasterCard* (along with whatever you can manage to squeeze out of good old mom and dad), but if you do not learn the art of funding your film career is going to be very short.

Believe me, I know what I'm talking about. I've watched too many talented filmmakers pack up their cars and leave town because they were hocked up to their eyeballs. It's not easy to produce a film when you're working all day at Kinko's and tending bar on the weekends so you can pay off the debt from your last project.

There is another reason why the funding stage is so critical. The very heart of your film begins with the funding process. The tasks you complete during the funding stage will take you deeper into your project than ever before. Your project will start to come together and will take on a whole new prospective as you explore and write about the background of your story, the style and structure you will use to tell the story, and all the other elements that go into your proposal. Dov S-S Simens of HollywoodU.com thinks funding is such an important part of the filmmaking process that he gave it its own special category, which he calls the "pre-preproduction" stage.

Too many filmmakers think the process of funding their films is going to be a long uphill battle that is going to suck the creative juices right out of their veins. Maybe this is because they can hear the dull echo of doors slamming before they even get started.

The money is out there. You just have to know how to find it. No, I haven't been living in a cave. I know times are tough. I have heard the grim economic forecasts. I have sat through meetings where board members drone on and on about how the economy has dramatically affected funding for the arts. Okay, so let's take a look at the figures and see just how bad things really are:

- According to the *Foundation Center*, U.S. Non-profit foundations donated approximately $29 billion in 2001. $3.7 billion of this went directly into the arts and culture.[i]
- A report by David Rockefeller's foundation, *Business Committee for the Arts (BCA)* said individuals, foundations, and corporations donated close to $11.5 billion to the arts, culture, and humanities in 2000.[ii]
- A follow-up poll by the *BCA* revealed that a majority of the companies recognized for supporting the arts said their level of giving in 2003 would remain consistent with their level of giving in 2002.[iii]

A report by the National Endowment for the Humanities (NEH) released the following breakdown of these statistics:

Amount given by U.S. foundations
2001 $29 billion estimate
2000 $27.6 billion

Amount given by Corporate foundations
2001 $3.1 billion estimate
2000 $3 billion

Amount received by Arts and humanities organizations
2000 $441.1 million
1999 $407.5 million

Amount received by Media Organizations:
2000 $224.8 million
1999 $174.6 million

Amount granted for film video and radio programs:
2000 $103.3 million
1999 $100 million

Ford foundation support for arts media and communications:
2000 $98.1 million
1999 $68.3 million from the Ford Foundation

Ford Foundation Grants for Documentaries:
2002 $3.4 million
2001 $3.4 million

NEA GRANTS Issued to Arts and TV Productions
2001 $3.8 million
2000 $3 million

NEH grants issued to Documentary Productions
2001 $7.4 million
2000 $4.7 Million

Now, how much did you say it was going to take to get your film made and distributed? We are talking *billions* of dollars here! *Individuals and corporations are giving away billions of dollars to support the arts.* The amount you need to make your film represents a tiny drop in the bucket, so what's stopping you from going out there and getting your piece of the funding pie?

If you believe your film is worth the effort and the money that it is going to take to produce it, and if you believe that you have what it takes to become a great filmmaker, then you owe it to yourself to take the journey toward discovering the art of funding your films. Along the way I will introduce you to ideas and concepts that I have picked up after more than 30 years in the film industry.

Throughout this book you will also hear from successful industry professionals who will share insights and strategies that will help you make your filmmaking dreams a reality.

Just one more thing before we take off. I travel light. There's no room for negativity on this train so you are going to have to leave your excess baggage at the station!

Carole Joyce

May Peace Prevail on Earth

Chapter

1

COMMIT OR BE COMMITTED

*The guideposts or books will only tell you the road or the
direction for the destination. You must make the journey and
experience the joy and the victory.* -Sai Baba

You've got an idea for a film. Great! So does my neighbor's daughter, the man who sold me this computer, and the pizza delivery boy. My plumber pitched a film that will gross ten times more than E.T. while he unclogged my sink!

So what sets your idea apart from the rest of the naked city's untold stories? What makes your story so special that investors and grantors are going to want to hand you their hard earned money and let you take it to Tinseltown to produce a film?

I've read grant applications that start off, "I am thinking about making a film about the secret lives of moths. What do you think?" Even if the concept was crackerjack, the filmmaker's lack of confidence and commitment to the project makes me (along with every funder I know) nervous enough to pass.

With that in mind, I have devised a list of questions that every potential filmmaker should answer before committing to a project. This is not one of those *Cosmo* quizzes where you add up all the "A's" and "B's" and subtract all the "C's" to get some arbitrary score. If you answer each question honestly your answers will reveal your level of commitment to the film.

1. List three compelling reasons why this film should be made.

2. Describe your connection to the story and explain why you are the one who should make this film.

3. Who will benefit from this film? If your primary purpose in making the film is to prove that you can do it, then that's what you should put down. Just be honest.

4. Are you willing to quit your job for the next three years and accept the financial consequences that will accompany this decision?

5. If not, can you produce the film in your spare time?

6. How many hours a week can you put into this film?

7. Are you willing to give up your family time to do this film?

8. Are you willing to forgo the Gap and wear the same clothes for the next 3 years?

9. How long can you drive your car? Will it last the next 3 years with minor repairs?

10. Why is this film important to you?

You should now have a healthy concept of the reality of filmmaking. If your answers tell you that this is not the film you are willing to make these sacrifices for then don't do it. If, however, your answers reflect that you are willing to make the sacrifices necessary to make this film, that you are fully committed to your project and nothing can stop you, then read on, this book was written just for you.

Of course that doesn't mean this is going to be a cakewalk. Producing an independent film is a lot like draining an alligator pit. Most of the time you are so busy fighting off alligators that it's easy to forget why you went in there in the first place! That's why you're going to carry your answers with you where ever you go. When things get hairy take them out and read them again. Remember where you are coming from and focus on that energy.

Secrets to Success

The Soul never thinks without a mental picture.
—Aristotle

Two equally talented filmmakers set off to make their fortunes. One ends up securing a three-picture deal at *Miramax* while the other ends up parking cars in West Covina. What is the key ingredient that separates these two filmmakers? Is it film school? I doubt it since the majority of successful filmmakers out there did not graduate from film school. Is it wealth? Hardly.

Try creativity and vision.

"Cool Carole! I've got creativity! I've got vision!"

I'm sure you do grasshopper, but stay with me. Successful filmmakers know how to apply their creativity to the *entire* project, from the first spark of an idea, all the way through preproduction, production, distribution, and screening. Successful filmmakers understand that funding their project is as much an art as producing it.

My good friend Lynn Preston, who lives outside Sai Baba's compound in Puttaparthi, India, told me a beautiful story about the power of visualization. One afternoon while Sai Baba and several men were engaged in a planning meeting, Sai Baba pointed to a site on the map and announced that they would build a hospital with a new school and a new housing complex close by. When one of the men interrupted Sai Baba and asked him where the money was going to come from, Sai Baba looked at the man and simply said, "from where ever it is now."

That is such a simple way to manifest. Sai Baba did build the hospital, the school and the housing complex. He brought the money from where ever it was at that time into his coffers and created his dreams. This is a key element to manifesting money. Don't worry about where the money for your film will come from, just know that it will come to you from some bank, from some corporation, or "from where ever it is now." Once you make the decision that your film must be made and that you are the right person to make it, see and feel that money in your bank account.

The Journey

It is our duty as men and women to proceed as though the limits of our abilities do not exist.
—Pierre Teihard de Chardin

The journey starts upstairs in your head. You must be ready to throw away any preconceived ideas about the funding process. The economic forecasters were right. Times have changed—there is more money than ever! You just have to learn to go outside the box and look for it. That is what this book is about. It is about adopting new ways of thinking when it comes to funding your film. It is about recreating some of the old methods and accepting new ones.

That's exactly what documentary filmmaker Nina Gilden Seavey did when she decided to do a documentary about seven Russian teenagers who formed a country western band called Bering Strait. Nina took her idea to *PBS* who had embraced several of her films in the past, only this time the execs at *PBS* sent her away without a dime and Nina found herself out there dancing on a high wire without a net. She could have given up on her idea. She could have come up with another project that *PBS* would accept, but after some deep soul searching she knew that she had to make this film. Instead of accepting defeat Nina decided *PBS*'s rejection would be a new beginning. Once she came to this decision she started searching for alternative ways to make her dream a reality.

It didn't take long. While reading the trades one morning Nina discovered that Roland House had just taken a multi-million dollar leap into the HD arena. This gave her an idea. She needed equipment and backing, and she knew

Roland House could use a documentary shot on HD as an effective marketing tool. But when Nina sat down to prepare her pitch she realized that she had very little to offer. She wanted to shoot the film cinéma vérité style and knew this meant the project could take years to produce. Now this would have put most filmmakers off, but Nina came up with an approach.

She put together a proposal that was honest and realistic. She knew that she could not guarantee the success of her proposed venture so she offered Roland House what she had. She offered her full attention and commitment to the project along with her promise that she would keep their best interest in mind at all times. As a seasoned producer and director, Nina knew that her reliability throughout this project, and her reputation for reliability during past productions was the best asset she had.

After Nina won support from Roland House she took her creativity on location to Russia where she made cold calls to Russian oil companies in search of additional support. She didn't let the language barrier or the gruff foreigners on the other end of the line intimidate her. She kept at it until she found an oil baron who listened. When she finished her pitch he presented her with an unusual proposition. He would donate money for her film if she could get Bering Strait to play at his birthday party. Nina worked with the band's manager, delivered the band at the appropriate place and time, and true to the oil baron's word her check came in the mail. Nina also used more traditional methods to drawing attention to her work, which had some odd and unexpected results.

Bering Strait was selected for the *No Borders Independent Feature Film Market* sponsored by the *IFP*. There was a lot of interest, but no one was willing to help with the financing (at that time, or ever as it turned out). But oddly enough, the same weekend Nina was at *No Borders*, a 13-minute work-in-progress of her film was being screened at the *Jackson Hole Digital Fusion Symposium*. There was so little hi-def material being shot at the time that the symposium organizers asked to screen her work even though the project wasn't finished. Nina couldn't attend the *Jackson Hole Symposium* as she was in New York at the *IFP*, but Barry Rebo, one of the pioneers of hi-def, was there. When he saw Nina's project he knew she would need financing for her doc so he called her and offered to act as her agent and co-producer. Barry was able to negotiate an agreement with *NHK* in Japan, whose Hi-Vision service is at the forefront of broadcast distribution of HD material. So while nothing came out of the weekend at the *IFP* in New York as Nina had hoped, there were obviously other forces at work elsewhere to help her get this film made.

Nina carried her creativity all the way through to an unforgettable screening. The final credits rolled to an end and the screen went black bathing the theatre in darkness. Suddenly the audience went wild. The same seven Russian teenagers they had just followed in Nina's 98-minute heart-tugging documentary walked out from behind the projection screen and started playing *The Ballad of Bering Strait*. Nina won the Audience Award at the *2002 Washington DC Film Festival* and won the *Official Selection* at the *International Documentary Association Festival in Los Angeles*, and *Bering Strait* was nominated for a Grammy.

But Nina wasn't out of the woods yet. She had wracked up a $250,000 debt in fees and services to *Roland House* and license fees from music publishers. Nina finished the film but she obviously was going to need a large sale.

Barry introduced Nina to Ira Deutchman, famed founder and former president of *Fine Line Features*. Ira loved the project and using a very carefully developed strategy, he proved all of the marketing gurus wrong who had predicted that no one would buy a movie about an unknown country music band from Russia. *Emerging Pictures, Microsoft, Digital Cinema Solutions* and *Country Music Television* sponsored the theatrical release of Ballad. The film sold to *VIACOM* for VH1/CMT for broadcast, and the DVD rights were sold as the first release on the *Koch-Lorber* DVD Label of *Koch Entertainment*, plus the film is now represented by *3-DD Entertainment* in London for foreign sales!

Nina Seavey is a filmmaker who knows the art of filmmaking involves the entire filmmaking process. Once you move to this concept your natural creativity will open up a floodgate of fundraising ideas.

I want you to recapture your childlike faith that will enable you to see, hear, and feel your goals. When I was a kid I listened to a radio program called *Let's Pretend.* Every Saturday morning I would tune in my radio and take off on a wonderful exotic trip. I never left my home but you could never tell me that. As far as I was concerned I was right there alongside Miss Nila Mack and her cast of Pretenders on every one of their magical voyages.

I'm sure you have similar memories of playing make-believe. Remember how real it all seemed?

When I want something I put it in writing first. This helps me clarify what it is I really want. Begin by writing down your goals. Describe exactly what you want to do and what the outcome will be. Draw pictures if you like, just include as much detail as you possibly can.

Once you have outlined your funding goals get a mental picture of how you will fund it. Picture your bank account with a large balance and see the date.

See a check with a large amount of money and see yourself depositing it you're your account. Visualize your dream by believing that the money is coming from a specific place- a bank, a generous philanthropist, a corporation-wherever it is now. Believing will open your mind and allow you to continue without being blocked by fear.

Next, verbalize your dream. Discuss it with someone close, taking great care to describe your dream or goal exactly as you see it. The more detail you use the better, because detail helps you visualize exactly what you want. This is how you empower your dreams.

Start with an idea.

Write it down.

Visualize.

Verbalize.

There are two books that will help you with this part of your journey. *Excuse Me, Your Life is Waiting For You: The Astonishing Power of Feelings*, by Lynn Grabhorn, will help you master the art of visualization, while T*he Four Agreements: A Practical Guide to Personal Freedom*, by Don Miguel Ruiz, will help you overcome the self-limiting beliefs that plague so many of us.

Throughout my career in the industry I have witnessed the success of some very strange films while excellent projects fell by the wayside. This led me to the realization that there is a missing ingredient in filmmaking that is not spoken of within industry circles. I first believed the missing ingredient was passion, then I looked deeper and saw that many filmmakers who found themselves blocked halfway through production had plenty of passion. Some were so dedicated they were working sixty hours a week so they could scrape together the funds to complete their film, but it still wasn't happening for them. No, passion is an important ingredient, but it is not the *secret* ingredient.

Lynn Grabhorn found the missing ingredient I was looking for. Her book will help you understand how we attract the very things we feel: fear, worry, guilt, self-doubt-you know, those issues that are usually foremost in a filmmaker's mind? "Did I choose the right format?" "Should I have gone with the more experienced editor?" "Am I going to be able to pull off the pitch of a lifetime when I walk through that door?"

These books will help you understand why many of your dreams have not materialized and they will give you the tools to change your life. They will help you cleanse your mind and prepare you for the *Art of Funding Your Film.*

The Power of Sounds and Words

The thought that comes from your mind should be pure; the words you utter should be true and sweet and the work you do should be sacred.

—Sai Baba

It was a perfect day in the Bahamas. The air was clear and the 80-degree water below offered amazing visibility. As I dove off the platform of Martin Woolen's grand yacht, the *Mustard Seed*, I was greeted by a kaleidoscope of comical fish along with an amazing assortment of exotic creatures, all coexisting amid a spectacular coral garden. It was a sight that soothed the soul.

I was joyfully exploring this underwater wonderland when another guest from the yacht swam toward me pointed out a giant lobster, then without warning, aimed his spear gun and sent his spear into the tail of the brightly colored creature. The lobster emitted an ear-piercing scream as it writhed about. I will never forget that sound; it taught me the awesome power of sound to convey emotions.

Many creatures emit sounds or change colors to express themselves, and the octopus is one of the greatest of the underwater communicators. When they are hungry they change colors to disguise themselves from unsuspecting prey, when they feel sexy they change colors to attract a mate, and when threatened they change colors to confuse their enemy. It seems for the octopus every single thought is on display in living color! The octopus is so talented that he can even emit a cloud of black ink that resembles his own shape, a phenomenon called pseudomorph, meaning false body.

We also become what we believe. You are a very unique being. Look at the talents you possess and cherish yourself. *Never ever* put yourself down. My father, Roy W. Dean, used to say, "if you can't say something nice about a person, don't say anything at all." This proverb also applies to what you say about yourself. You have been chosen to impart art, beauty, and knowledge to the rest of us. Everything you do is a reflection of you. If you put yourself down you also put down your film, so hold yourself in the highest esteem.

The words we use to describe our dreams and our aspirations hold an immense power to create and manifest. Think about the words you use to create things in your life. How many times have you made plans for the future and verbalized your plans? Once spoken, your plans are like a *fait accompli*. What you have said comes true even if you are not aware that you verbalized this plan in the past. Be responsible and choose your words carefully when verbalizing your hopes and dreams. Above all, be kind to yourself.

As an artist you also have a profound responsibility to choose the best sounds and words to project your message. Your audience will walk away from your film with images embedded in their senses. Once you show something as fact many people will store this information forever and it will become part of their belief system.

Alison Landsberg coined the phrase *prosthetic memory*, to describe a phenomenon that occurs when memories that are not organically based, are nonetheless experienced with one's own body through various cultural technologies, such as film and television. According to Landsberg the experience of film, "might actually install in individuals 'symptoms' through which they didn't actually live, but to which they subsequently have a kind of experiential relationship." Landsberg's studies have shown that prosthetic memories derived from watching films can actually "become part of one's personal archive of experience."[iv]

If you move to the concept that you are shaping minds and assigning emotions and beliefs with every picture, every word, and every sound, you will realize how important your words, sounds, and pictures are to humanity. This is especially true when pictures are enhanced with words, sounds, and music. You must be in control of your script and take great care during the edit if your audience is going to receive the message you want them to receive.

You should always be asking, "do these words convey the message I am trying to impart to the world?" "Do the sounds convey the meaning and emotions I want my audience to remember?"

Sound is one of the most powerful tools you will use in your film. Sound can create and sound can destroy. It can shatter glass, and can even produce subtle patterns in sand. Sound can lower or increase blood pressure. When martial arts experts shout "KI-AI!" during impact, they are using sound to focus all of their internal energy. *Kiai*, also known as the spirit yell, literally means to concentrate one's life force or energy.

There is a scene in *Bobby Deerfield* when the film's terminally ill heroin waits for a noisy train before she releases the most unforgettable scream. The entire theatre can feel this woman's anger, grief, despair, and helplessness. I was so impressed that I went home and tried to do the same thing. I put on a CD, cranked it up full-blast, then let it rip. It was very disappointing. All I could manage to come up with was a squeaky stifled little shriek. I immediately went to work on improving my scream and can now go up against some of the best screamers out there. Sound strange? Try it! I find it amazingly therapeutic and frequently will use it to release all sorts of pent-up emotions. Of course this therapy should be used with caution as it can elicit some strange looks, not to mention a police officer or two at your front door!

Sound conveys energy and meaning to your audience. It is up to you to make sure it conveys the meaning you want to project.

31

The absence of sound can be just as powerful. There is not one word on the promo for Lee Lew Lee's documentary, *Downwinders*, yet the message is burned on your subconscious through powerful visuals and haunting silence.

Lee Lew Lee has a remarkable ability to produce factual films that entertain and inspire. After winning his Roy W. Dean Film Grant he went on to produce one of the best exposes on the '60's I have ever seen. *All Power to the People* gives amazing insight into what really happened during this tumultuous era. Broadcast in over 30 nations on 12 different networks, *All Power to the People* has influenced millions of people. Audiences walk away from this film with newfound knowledge of the Black Panther movement. They also walk away inspired and hopeful.

Film is a powerful medium and you can use this power to manifest a positive change. Please use your gift wisely. Leave your audience with solutions, not despair.

Jack London once said, "You can't wait for inspiration. You have to go after it with a club." That is exactly how Xachery Irving made

A CONVERSATION WITH
Filmmaker, Xackery Irving

American Chain Gang, *a documentary that explores the controversial revival of prison chain gangs in the South. Xackery is a hunter. He is always moving; always observing. He stalks the human condition with a camera and takes deliberate dead aim on his subjects to produce documentaries that make a difference.*

In a recent interview I chatted with Xackery about how he captured the idea for American Chain Gang, *how he raised the funds, and how he managed to stay focused while surrounded by such a hostile environment.*

Xackery, I heard that after *American Chain Gang* was released, the practice of using chain gangs was actually outlawed in Georgia. Where do you get your ideas, and how did you decide on your subject matter?

Sometimes people find ideas from conversations or from something they read. What sparked me was a photo essay on the chain gang in Alabama. It had beautiful black and white photos of the officers and the inmates and it really stirred me. I thought this is an experience that hasn't been around for years. I researched it thinking of making a film. I focused on prior works and found some short news stories on the subject. During the research of the history of chain gangs I found horrible things that were done to inmates. Releasing them to coal mines and factories where they were forced to work under harsh conditions, no heat, chained to beds without mattresses, and no medical attention whatsoever.

I had an interesting perspective of this concept and I felt it was a very powerful subject. I took a trip to Alabama and received permission to spend time at the prison and meet people who would be in the film and then I was hooked. I knew this was a good story. I saw inmates that were white

33

supremacists chained to and working with African Americans. I saw the resentment and hatred among the inmates that were chained together and I saw the resentment from the inmates to the officers. This seemed to be an emotionally charged environment. I felt I could tell the story.

It's an amazing process to watch the story unfold, isn't it?

When I was in Alabama, I called you Carole and you gave me some ideas on production. You said, "this film is its own animal. It will take on its own life and you will have to follow it. It is a live being now and it will take its own path." You said, "you can contribute your own vision, but you have to catch this reality and it can be refreshing that you don't have control of some things."

You have the luxury of catching these elements of reality with a net. It is like building a house versus building a prefab home or a skyscraper with your budget. You have a blue print of what you want to build and it is very well planned. Next you get the things you need to build with, your script, your coverage, and you have a strong idea of the film based on the blue print. Doc filmmaking in this analogy is finding trees to make a log cabin but in production you are gathering these logs and cutting them down and when you go to the edit suite, that's where you really make the film. These raw materials now exist and you can't design them. You have to put them together. You may think you have an idea, but once you get into the edit room your story is what you have on the film.

How did you go about making your dream a reality? How did you get the ball rolling?

The most important thing you need to do for the film is to be very organized. You need to have a good treatment, a solid pitch and a clear presentation of what you want to achieve in the film.

Having a well-written treatment is most important. If you can get press clippings about the subject matter, and press about you making this film, it will be very helpful. Have all of this in a presentable book and include your budget information too. Being prepared to answer questions about the film in a clear and definitive way will show people that you are very close to the subject and are fully organized.

So the search for funding begins.

I applied for the Roy W. Dean grant in New York because I knew that I could make the film. Once I was chosen as one of the five finalists, I heard I had to pitch the film in front of an audience. Now I had to create a verbal pitch to give at the National Arts Club in front of filmmakers. This made me get even closer to the film.

The night Xackery pitched his film at the National Arts Club, he and Ann Stern were neck and neck for first place. The judges were going back and forth, agonizing over the decision before finally awarding the grant to Stern.

Xackery did not walk away with first place that night but it was far from over for this tenacious filmmaker. His passion and dedication to his project really came through in his pitch, which is why I decided then and there to find a way to help him realize his dream. I dug some ASA 50 16 mm stock out of the vault and donated it to him so he could start shooting.

It really does all start with the concept and the pitch, doesn't it? What advice can you give filmmakers about pitching their projects?

It is good to practice your pitch. You will be asking a lot of people to help with your film, so learn how to pitch your film and ask for help so even if they say no it is never a waste of time. You can look at it as practice to help you to sharpen your pitch.

The other good thing about talking to people-pitching to people-is that it forces you to be very articulate about the direction of the film, as people ask questions on the film. It becomes a good process to listen to ideas from others and go over logistical problems. This prepares you mentally and creates new approaches for how and what to shoot.

What is the most difficult challenge when approaching potential donors?

You have to be very clear about what they are contributing to. If you are asking for time or money you have to have a clear concise picture of what you want to do in your film so they are clear about what they are providing. You always want to know exactly what you want to ask for.

Documentaries are special in this way as they are usually films that have a social issue or they are something about people or the world that takes times to achieve. You are selling a film about something that you have to examine. You want to help change the world through this examination. This can be very powerful. When you communicate this with enthusiasm it can be contagious. You want to ignite the same spark in the donor.

So there you were with your vision and some donated raw stock. How did you keep the momentum moving forward?

I believe you must start shooting. Do what you have to do to get the resources together so you can start shooting. It is very effective to cut a 5-minute piece to communicate the ideas of your film and what your story is about in a compressed format. This is also another way of making your pitch visually. You are communicating what your editorial style will be, who your characters are and what your creative approach is. You can put this on paper until the cows come home but you will have a much greater response when it is on film. It is a financial burden but it is the most effective way to get things off the ground. As soon as you are prepared mentally just start shooting so you have visual material to present to your donors and grantors.

Another mentor of mine is George Stoney who is now in his 80's. He is a wonderful man who teaches documentary filmmaking at NYU. He has made several docs and is called the grandfather of public access. He is another great documentary filmmaker who has his door open to anyone. When George read *American Chain Gang's* treatment he told me it is really tough to raise money with paper. You have to shoot something to show them your vision.

When you were filming *American Chain Gang*, you were one-on-one with some pretty tough characters. What advice can you offer other documentary filmmakers about how to approach the interview?

Your subjects are the people who communicate your story. It's great to have articulate people but you don't always have this luxury. There are times you have to use people that are not good communicators. This becomes a challenge. Know that everyone is an interesting person even if there may be lots of digging involved to find it. Look for interesting parts of their personality that work well with your story and makes them sympathetic to the viewer. This is a process of uncovering parts of a personality that at first glance may not read well on camera. Sitting down and getting to know them is a good way to find interesting elements for your film.

How do you win your subject's trust, especially inside a prison?

You need to get them used to the camera. They are in a very vulnerable position, putting themselves in your hands. Let them look through the viewfinder and roll some film on you. Let the subject of the film be empowered to tell their own story. If you impose your storytelling on them too much they will feel this and you will not get an organic story. If they feel and know they have the ability to express themselves in their own words then you have opened the treasure chest and will find some gems you never considered.

What important lessons have you learned about the art of the interview?

Albert Maysles taught me that it is more effective to have someone communicate an idea to someone else in the film rather than to the camera. It allows the audience to see the information unfold between two people so it seems more organic and real.

Good docs are about people. Whether you are making a social issue film or one about a character. The most compelling thing to people is a story of someone's experience. The camera changes everything when it is there and it is a wonderful tool to gather your story with nothing between your subject and the lens. You have to be fast and open your mind and heart to tell the story as it unfolds.

If you had the opportunity to go back and do this film over again what would you do differently?

I would have fewer subjects. I would spend more time with my subjects to get them comfortable with the camera. I would stay glued to them to get their story. I would get more interactions between the main character and other people. I would have communicated more conflicts between them, and I will do that in my next film.

You want a human face to tell your story. The most compelling thing in a film is people overcoming conflict and obstacles to get what they want.

As a documentary filmmaker you are constantly shooting life as it unfolds. What tips can you offer new filmmakers?

This is a great way to tell a story. It is like hunting; you get the shot or you don't. If you are not comfortable with shooting then hire someone. The wonderful thing about it is the more you shoot and are in this environment you will begin to anticipate how the action will come across and you can get into position.

Ask yourself these questions before each scene:

"Do I have the camera in the right position?" There may be more than one correct position. You have to think of yourself as a war photographer and get close to the action.

"Do I have depth of field?"

"Is my sound coming through clearly?"

"Is it more important to follow the action or is important to be in position to get the elements that are there?"

You have to judge changing camera positions and the position of your mike while the scene is happening because there is no second take.

"Are the right questions being asked?"

"Is the objective of the scene being clearly communicated?"

"Am I getting the material that my editor and I will need in the editing suite to tell this story-a variety of angles, different camera positions, different focal lengths that will cut well together?"

If you are not a professional cinematographer hold shots longer than you think you need to. We may know where to cut in our heads but you have to hold longer than you want to look at the shot. You may find something magical just when you were about to turn off; you might even find a good audio clip at the end.

Are you getting a beginning, middle and an end of each scene? Many times you will turn a camera on as the scene has begun. You need to think of how you can set that scene up. You may want your subject to enter the room. It is important to have a visual and audio for the beginning and get some options for the editor.

The end of the scene may be as easy as someone leaving the room or the frame or the conversation ending. Many times you can find other endings and you want them so that you will have options in the editing room. It is important to keep this process in your mind as you are shooting, keep asking yourself these questions and you will become a good shooter and editor.

Xackery, you really hit the mark with *American Chain Gang*. It's full of amazing contrasts. The drab colors of the prison against the rich colors of the countryside that surround it. As I watched this film I could feel myself being drawn into the subjects lives. I could feel the despair of being chained together and working while surrounded by such beauty.

I am so happy I shot *Chain Gang* on film. On a visual level the film needed that vibrant image of the gang chained together.

Yet you've said that your next film will probably be shot on digital.

You can tell a story with one person with a digital but it is very difficult to do a one-person film shoot. There are lots of advantages with a small crew. You can be very mobile quickly and you don't affect the environment when you have one or two people in the crew.

Also it is a great idea to look at your footage and listen to your audio as soon as you can. Video lets you do this immediately. Film must be processed while on location. You need to see where you can improve while on location. Look for what is working and what did not work. It gives you confidence and you can pick up what you lost. Get a head start on the editing, if you see things you missed you can get them next time. Editing will always show you where the holes are. When you view your dailies you can see what your options are and what footage you have to tell the story. Give your editor options and you will have a great story.

I use a small DV camera, which gives me flexibility. You can monitor your audio and shoot at the same time. This gives you more intimacy with your subject and is the key to making you as close to invisible as possible. You can see how the subject reacts to your big crew versus a small crew. It changes the way you tell the story.

Xackery, what do you like best about being a documentary filmmaker?

I love the process of filmmaking. Making documentaries is terrific because it is hands-on. You can start anytime you want. It is as simple as picking up the tape and camera and following people around. You can light or not light, as you choose. You can bring material to editing and start your film immediately. I love storytelling and I love shooting, editing, and planning scenes. Ever since the first day in film school when I shot something and saw it on the screen this has stayed with me.

Is film school a must?

Film school is not imperative. What it does is give you a level of training and this can give you a false sense of confidence, thinking that you can make a film right away.

So what is the prerequisite to becoming a good filmmaker?

41

You need a strong sense of confidence to start this process as films are very demanding emotionally, financially, and creatively. They demand all you have and docs can be shot over a course of years. You must be in love with the process.

It is a benefit to choose the people you work with because you can foster life long relationships with these people and it can be rewarding. You want to find a great editor who you can create with and who is a good listener. The editor/director relationship in a film is so very important. I prefer to work with an editor, rather than edit myself because editors can take your material in directions you never considered. A good editor will listen to your ideas and come up with a direction you may have missed. What a treat this is. Getting the right editor is as important as raising money. Don't look just for talent, look for someone you can communicate with and like. Remember, the editor is your first audience. You don't want to let them down. You need to get the material they need to make your film.

Do you have any parting words of encouragement to fellow filmmakers out there in the trenches?

Be easy on yourself. Shooting and editing can be difficult and draining. You may miss things each day and make mistakes. You will be under the gun constantly. This is all part of the process. We all experience this. Just keep forging ahead and you will find a way to tell your story in the process. Take it easy on yourself and have the faith to know your film will be finished one way or the other.

THE PERFECT PITCH

*Playing without the fundamentals is like eating
without a knife and fork. You make a mess.*
—**Dick Williams**

I don't know how the word pitch first became synonymous with the art of describing a film but it seems appropriate. The film pitch is like the baseball pitch in that it is critical to the outcome of the game. While it is the pitcher's job to get the ball over the base it is actually the catcher's job to tell the pitcher what kind of ball to throw.

Your catcher is your investor or your funder. If you pay attention to your catcher you will have a better chance of winning the game. You know that you might have to adjust the speed and the trajectory a little here and a little there, depending upon whom your pitching to, but the goal remains the same: *you've got to connect the ball with the glove.* To do this you are going to have to create a pitch that will sell and you are going to have to work on it until it is perfect. This is one of the most important steps in *The Art of Funding your film.*

In the appendix you will find a list of funders. Don't even think about getting up there on the mound and going after these funders until you have perfected your pitch.

Go back to the questions that every potential filmmaker should answer in chapter one and expound upon your answers to the first three questions:

1. List three compelling reasons why this film should be made.
2. Describe your connection to the story and explain why you are the one who should make this film.

3. Who will benefit from this film?

4. What is the urgency?

Next, write about the concept of your film. Keep writing until you run out of steam then walk away and let it sit for at least a day.

Sometimes when you start writing you open up a flood-gate of creativity. Keep a little notebook in your pocket during the day and on your nightstand when you go to bed so you can jot down ideas as they come. Remember, an un-written idea is an unfinished idea.

Now go back to your notes and edit everything down to two paragraphs or less. Your pitch must convey the meaning of your film while capturing all the passion, intrigue, drama, or humor of your story. It must move the audience and leave them wanting more.

Writing a pitch is like writing poetry or the lyrics to a song. Use words that will use the utmost compression, force, and economy. As you work on your pitch read it out loud. How does it sound? Does it roll off your tongue or does it sound clumsy? Rewrite it, read it out loud, then rewrite it again. Keep working on it until the words have just the right rhythm and pace.

Your pitch may be the only chance you get to tell someone about your film. You may find yourself standing next to the head of *Sundance* acquisitions at a crowded cocktail party, or you may find out that the grumpy little old lady sitting next to you on the plane is a wealthy entrepreneur who got bumped to coach. You may be up against some heavy hitters so make sure you are always ready with your perfect pitch.

The Wind-up and Delivery

You need to have the same level of confidence when you pitch to Sheila Nevins at HBO that you have when you pitch to your best friend. This confidence will come with practice and from knowing with complete certainty that you are presenting a great story that people are going to be interested in.

You and your pitch need to become inseparable. Write it down and carry it with you. Stick it in your purse or backpack. Sew a special little pocket for it in your swimsuit, just don't leave home without it. I want you to whip it out wherever you are and practice. Practice it on the bus driver. Practice it on your doctor's receptionist. Practice it on your imaginary friend while you're stuck in traffic.

- Give individual one-on-one pitch sessions to every one in your family and be sure to write down their comments and questions. As you pitch your story pay close attention to how they respond and listen to what they say.
- Are they excited about the story?
- Do they act like they want to know more?
- Does your pitch stir up interest and stimulate questions?

Remember, potential donors are likely to ask some of the same questions that your family and friends ask. Don't forget to research and follow-up on all of their questions so you can be ready with good answers. If a question is asked repeatedly consider addressing the issue in your pitch.

No matter how hard you prepare you will come up against some questions that you don't have the answer for. Just be honest. Explain that you are still in preproduction and that you have not worked out all the details yet. Try to anticipate challenging questions and don't be afraid to memorize your answers.

Your project is still in its infancy. This is the critical stage when everything will start to come together, so pay attention. Sometimes pitching your project will bring you some great ideas. That's what Xackery Irving discovered when he pitched his idea for *American Chain Gang.* The more he pitched the more feedback he got. He listened and ended up using several ideas that evolved out of discussions from his pitch.

Practice your pitch and practice your answers until your delivery is smooth and convincing. Become one with your pitch. Memorize it until it's part of your DNA.

This is the beginning of funding your film.

After several weeks of pitching your project to friends, patient family members, and complete strangers, your pitch will feel as comfortable as your favorite pair of blue jeans. Your pitch will be on a much higher level and will contain the elements that will capture the interest of anyone you speak to.

Remember, it is a good pitch if:

1. It is entertaining.
2. You enjoy it.
3. You believe it.
4. It makes your project exciting and desirable.
5. It communicates how your film will make a difference.
6. It creates a sense of urgency.
7. It works and you get funded!

Your vision will become clear only when you can look into your own heart....Who looks outside, dreams; who looks inside, awakes.

—*Carl Jung*

THE PROPOSAL

Reading proposals is a passion of mine, which is a good thing since I read over 500 proposals and view over 1000 corresponding tapes a year for my Roy W. Dean film grants. Filmmakers frequently ask me how they can improve their applications.

First, remember, sponsors are usually under a deadline to make a decision on something that should never be judged: your art. Your potential sponsor is probably reviewing hundreds of proposals, one right after the other, so find a way to make your proposal unique.

I consider the introduction or synopsis to be the most critical element in the proposal. It is the first thing I read when I pick up a new film proposal because it tells me how compelling the project is and reveals how passionate the filmmaker is. Sponsors use the synopsis during the selection process. If your synopsis is dynamic and is strategically placed on your application it will remain active in the sponsor's mind.

This is a visual industry, yet only ten percent of the applications I receive include pictures. This always amazes me. Since the person reading your proposal is probably very visual, consider dropping a few pictures or graphics into your proposal.

How about submitting a picture of yourself with your application? Include a photograph taken during your last film shoot—something that shows you in action, behind the camera or giving direction. Even if it's just your student ID, put that shining smile on the page and let us see who you are! Passion, perseverance, and personalization are what you need to win grants, so put your heart on your sleeve and win that grant!

How many grants have you entered? Tell us about them so we can see how determined you are to make this film. Do you really want this grant? Are you willing to dedicate the next three years of your life to produce this film? Find a way to communicate your dedication in your proposal. Include a personal film statement. Tell us what is driving you.

Remember:

Grantors want compelling film work.

The first two paragraphs must be dynamite.

Be impeccable with the truth. Sponsors know if your budget is unreasonable.

Do not commit to things you cannot do. Sponsors can tell when you are overstating.

A guaranteed audience, such as a commitment from PBS, puts you on top.

Demonstrate solid marketing, distribution plans, and outreach distribution.

Have you secured a distributor or another grantor?

Bringing a scholar or expert onboard will shift the scales to your advantage.

Show how your film relates to the goals of your potential sponsor or distributor.

Is your project one of a kind? If so explain this and include information to back up your statement.

If there are projects on the market with a similar message or subject matter to yours, make sure you demonstrate how yours is unique and how it compares.

Give specific information about your audience and include the full demographics.

Please, no hand written information on the proposal or the cover pages.

Attach letters from donors to your application.

Music and picture rights must go in the budget. They are expensive and donors will be looking for them.

Put your name and the name of your film on submitted tapes and on the outside of the video case. When donors are reviewing scores of tapes they often get interrupted and it's easy to confuse tapes.

Please don't use insulated bags that are lined with that horrid-gray-fluffy-stuff. We all hate them. Some donors won't even open these types of packages because the filaments can damage their VCRs. Plastic boxes and bubble wrap are a much better choice.

Mention creative fundraising ideas that you are using in your application. For example, filmmakers often barter with other filmmakers to get their projects completed. Donors like to see filmmakers who use creative funding techniques.

I usually call my finalists and discuss their film application. When possible I give them guidance and suggestions on how they can improve their proposal. The most important thing I tell them is to *submit again next year!*

The producers for the wonderful film, *The Flute Player*, applied three times before they won my Roy W. Dean Grant, but once they won they were on their way, subsequently winning a $50,000 Sundance grant and a PBS airing.

Winning one grant leads to success with future grants so mention prior grants that you have won in your cover letter.

Use a PR person to promote your accomplishments and you can easily pave the way for even more funding. I use Tory Berger for public relations and for promotion. He only takes spiritually based jobs and he is a pleasure to work with. You can contact Tory at: friends@netzero.net

49

Avoid using technical jargon in your application, and don't go into a lot of technical detail unless your proposal is directed to a grantor who has specifically asked for technical information. The people reading it will not know what a 20 to 1 zoom is nor will they recognize the latest digital camera you want to use. This can be confusing and divert them from the real issue of your film.

A funder who was speaking at a conference I recently attended told the audience about an applicant who entered her grant seven times! Each time the filmmaker asked the funder how he could improve his application. The filmmaker finally won on his seventh try. This is the kind of commitment every filmmaker needs.

If you have made mistakes there is always another chance for you . . . you may have a fresh start any moment you choose, for this thing we call "failure" is not the falling down, but the staying down.
—Mary Pickford

Once you start on your journey you are committed. Never give up. You may have to apply several times but don't despair. I tell filmmakers to stand by the Suffragette's motto, "Never Give Up!"

A CONVERSATION WITH
Writer/Filmmaker, Eva Hornbaker

When I came across JanEva Hornbaker's proposal during our Roy W. Dean New York Film Grant competition, I was struck by how well she managed to capture the heart of her story. I found her proposal to be exemplary and asked her if she would share her secrets for dynamic proposal writing.

Eva, what is the number-one rule of proposal writing?

The number-one rule of writing anything is to understand who your readers are and what you are trying to accomplish. This sounds like two rules but actually they are very integrated.

The film proposal is a tool designed to sell two things: your idea for a film, and your ability as a filmmaker to successfully produce, market, and distribute your film. You need to know everything you can about the organization you are applying to, and more specifically, the person who is going to read your proposal, if you are going to convince them to invest in you, which is what it always boils down to.

The funder's deadline is 3-weeks away. What are the first steps toward creating a perfect proposal?

The first step is to make sure your project fits the sponsor's funding guidelines. Once you have determined this you need to dig in and start researching the organization and the people behind the organization.

Read their mission statement and jot down key words and phrases used to describe the goals and objectives of the organization, then go to your proposal and try to use these same key words to describe your project. It's absolutely essential that you make a connection between the funder's goals and the goals of your project. This shouldn't be a stretch if your project is a good match with the funder.

Funders support interests that are closely tied to the source of their funds, so find out who is funding your funder. You can get this information right off their web site or from their tax return.

How did you go about organizing your proposal?

My education background is in library and information technology so I studied grant writing in college; however, when I went to write my first film proposal I found very little information that was geared specifically toward putting together an effective film proposal. I read everything I could find and researched a lot of different funders on the Internet and made a list of what each of these funders wanted, then I made my outline based on this list.

Did you find a lot of variation in what different funders wanted to see?

Oh yes. Some organizations only want a one-page synopsis while others want something that resembles a doctoral dissertation. I put together a general outline based on my research. That way I had all the information in one computer file. You are going to need all of this stuff anyway for distribution and marketing, so my advice is get it together early on, then customize it to each funder.

Customizing it is the key, isn't it?

Definitely. It's essential that you follow each funder's guidelines to the letter. If the funder doesn't ask for your budget, don't include it. If they want a two-page synopsis, make sure you only send two pages. And make sure you address each individual funder's goals and objectives.

Your proposal was very organized.

Funders want to be able to scan a proposal and immediately come away with information—what the film is about, the filmmaker's approach, style, goals, and objectives. They can do this if the proposal is organized into clear defined headings.

But you did not sacrifice style. Your proposal was not a dry analytical treatment. What can you share about how to achieve style in the proposal?

You have to give your reader all the information they need to make an informed decision, but how you say it is as important as what you say.

You are describing your ideas for a motion picture so it is essential that you *show* your reader instead of tell your reader what you intend to do. Ezra Pound said, "the image is more than an idea. It is a vortex or cluster of fused ideas and is endowed with energy." If you are going to energize a reader with your ideas then you have to do more than just describe your project; you need to actually transport your reader into your film.

Your opening paragraph does just that. Can you take us through the process of how you wrote this?

Sometimes when you're writing about something that you're passionate about it just flows, but this can be dangerous. It's critical not to miss any key ideas so I start by writing down exactly what it is that I need to communicate then I rewrite it adding descriptive words.

Could you take your opening paragraph here and breakdown the process?

Sure. I write the information I need to convey, which is:

World War II ended over five decades ago yet thousands of Americans are still missing.

As you can see this sentence provides information, but it does nothing to help the reader conjure up a visual picture. Like most filmmakers I think in pictures so I try to go back and rewrite the scene as I see it. One of my favorite writing teachers used to say, "Walk your reader through the corridors and hallways of your story." I think the best way to do this is to remove yourself from your story and approach it completely fresh, as though you've never been there.

You're so familiar with your story that it's easy to forget that the scenes are only in your head. You can't just say, "this story is about explorers who look for lost Americans," and expect your reader to see that fantastic scene that is in your head.

Close your eyes and picture the scene, then put it down on paper. Sometimes it helps to take the concept you are trying to describe and reduce it to one scene then work from there. You have to add physical detail because physical detail is going to pull your reader into the story.

So using this opening paragraph as an example, I worked in some descriptive words and ended up with:

The battlefields of World War II fell silent over five decades ago yet more than 78,000 young Americans still lie in shallow makeshift graves, rusting wrecks, and abandoned battlefields thousands of miles from home.

THE PROPOSAL

"Shallow makeshift graves" and "rusting wrecks" give the reader some very vivid pictures. "Young Americans," who could read that and remain unmoved? You have to describe your locations, describe your subject, and describe your subject's actions so the reader is transported into the scene. If I write:

This film will be shot in Europe and Asia as we follow searchers on different expeditions to find missing Americans.

Again, I've given the reader the information, but that's not my only objective here. I want to show the reader. So I add description and hopefully give it energy:

We will follow unique explorers across dramatic backdrops of Europe and into the deepest jungles of Asia as they search for the scattered bones and the rusted dog tags of young soldiers.

The trick to effective writing is to layer descriptive language with specific language so you don't end up with something that is too vague. You want to create mood but you don't want to over do it.

How do you know when it's too much?

When you sacrifice clarity for style you've gone too far. Funders don't want to read through tons of adjectives to get to the point. Make sure your proposal clearly demonstrates what your film is about and what you are trying to do. Save descriptive words to illustrate your subject, your location, your subject's motivation. Good writers control their style to match their purpose.

What is your biggest proposal writing challenge?

Knowing when to stop. When you're writing passionately about your subject it's tempting to keep going. Pretty soon you end up with something that resembles the Los Angeles phonebook.

I've received a few proposals that resembled phonebooks.

Once you've mastered the art of creating these wonderful paragraphs that draw the reader into the story, your next step is to chop it down to the minimum pages allowed. It's the hardest thing but it's a necessary part of the writing process. You just have to do this knowing that your best work is going to be what is left after you have eliminated all of the fluff and repetition.

William Strunk was really big on omitting needless words. He said, "Vigorous writing is concise," and he said "A sentence should contain no unnecessary words, a paragraph no unnecessary sentences." I think a lot of people think that omitting needless words means they need to cut down their sentences and paragraphs to the point where they sacrifice style, but this is not what he meant. Strunk went on to explain that you do not include unnecessary words and sentences, for the same reason that a drawing should have no unnecessary lines and a machine no unnecessary parts. You're not going to leave out an integral part of a drawing to make the drawing smaller. You're not going to leave off an essential bolt to make the machine lighter. Strunk said, "Make every word tell." That's a very powerful statement. I think most filmmakers can relate to this because this is the essence of good filmmaking. Make every scene tell.

So how do you stay on track?
The best way to stay on track is to work from a design. That way you're not going to veer off in a direction and write

about things that are not essential. Know exactly what you are trying to accomplish then develop an outline so you achieve all of your points.

I asked Eva to send me a sample of the outline she came up with after researching different funders. Use this guide as your standard outline and add additional elements according to each sponsor's requirements:

Introduction/Synopsis

Always start with your film statement or pitch. Make sure it includes the name of your film and describes exactly what your film is about. Keep this section short and passionate.

Background and Need

Acquaint the reader with essential information about the background of your story and your main characters. Don't bombard the reader with information. Give them just enough detail to capture their attention and motivate them to keep reading.

Next, explain why you want to do this film and why it will be of interest to others. What specific concerns will be addressed and why? Who will benefit and how? What will your film accomplish?

This is where you will insert the hook! You have already determined that your film fits the sponsor's guidelines for funding. Now carefully study the sponsor's mission statement and use it to create an original statement that demonstrates how your film relates to the sponsor's specific goals and priorities. This is a critical part of your proposal and it is something that most of your competitors will overlook.

Approach, Structure & Style

This is where you will describe how you are going to approach your story as a filmmaker.

Structure is the framework that holds up each element of your story. Describe how your story will unfold and how the subjects will move through each of these elements from beginning to end. Is your story an intimate personal journey or an expose? Are you going to use narration? Is there a connective thread that will tie all of the elements of the story together?

Sponsors want strong stories that have strong characters. How will your subjects relate to each other and how will they impact the story? Will your subjects experience personal growth? Will they help others grow? How will they carry the story forward through the conflict, the climax, and the final outcome? How will your audience react to the dramatic tension and what will they learn by the end of the story? Describe how your film will stir viewers to action and inspire them to make a difference.

If you are shooting life as it unfolds you may not know the final outcome. Explain this, then describe several possible outcomes and describe how you might approach each scenario. Remember, a story does not have to have a clear-cut solution to have resolution. An open-ended film that leaves unresolved issues can be even more compelling than a story that reveals how the lives of the characters or events turn out.

Style includes all of the techniques that will give your film its own unique quality or tone. This might include camera work, lighting techniques, or your interview style. Include everything that will project your personal imprint onto the story. Avoid getting lost in a lot of technical detail. Instead, explain (show) how a certain technique or style will be used to carry the story forward or illuminate a specific character.

Avoid describing one specific approach unless you have completed all of your research and are convinced there is only one way you can tell the story. Research can reveal twists and turns that can dramatically alter your approach, and changing approaches once a sponsor has already funded you can be sticky. If you are not committed to one approach, describe several approaches that you are exploring and explain how your subjects might respond to each of these approaches.

Coming up with an idea for a film is easy; nailing down the best approach is the hard part. If you have not decided on an approach, exploring and writing about different methods and ideas will draw you closer to your project.

Theme

The theme is what your story is about. If it is difficult to pinpoint an exact theme then your story is probably underdeveloped. Don't worry, dig deeper and do more research. Your theme will emerge as you continue to research and write.

When I first started researching the idea for *Searcher for Souls* I concentrated on how the ongoing consequences of war affects a family for generations. It was an important theme but I knew something was missing. It was only after I went to Europe and spent two months researching my subject that another theme began to unfold.

Philippe Castellano is a French explorer who has spent over 20 years searching for lost American flyers who fell from the sky during the Second World War. As I followed and observed my subject I began to notice remarkable similarities between Philippe and the young American flyers he was looking for.

My research trip to France led me to connections with other explorers from several different countries. My project quickly grew from a single one-off doc to a series of 5:1 hour programs, each featuring an explorer from a different country.

As I spent time with each explorer I discovered the amazing similarities that existed between the French explorer and the lost Americans was also present in the each of the foreign Searchers. Each Searcher's passion to find these missing Americans came from a deep conviction born from their past experiences, or those of their families. The Searchers, like the lost American's, answered a call and set out on the hero's journey. When I discovered this I knew I had found what was there all along, the thread that connected the elements of each story, and each story to the entire series.

As you research your story, don't forget to stand back and observe. Look for hidden themes that connect the elements of your story.

Audience, Marketing, and Distribution

Your sponsors will want to know about your intended audience. Is your film about a subject that has worldwide appeal? Do you plan to target a specific community? Is it educational or commercial? How will the market support your audience and how do you intend to distribute your film to this audience? Give statistics that support the size of your audience and explain how your film will appeal to this audience.

How have you approached distribution? Are you pursuing a specific network or cable television market? Does your film have a rental market? Will it be featured in public libraries, museums, or university collections? Will you enter your film in festivals? Sponsors want to see that you have a distribution plan and that you are exploring several options. Provide copies of letters of support from key individuals, networks, and anyone that can support the fact that your film will be seen.

Budget

Your budget must be a reasonable projection of how much it will cost to produce, distribute, and market your film. Make sure your budget is consistent with the production ideas you have described. Explain where you plan to come up with the rest of the funds to meet your budget.

This is also where you will describe how you will use the award if you should win.

Make sure you include a brief statement acknowledging the goals and objectives of the foundation and make it clear that you will use the award accordingly. Let the sponsor know how much you need this grant and that it will be used to create a film that will help advance their cause.

A film budget can have many hidden elements that can come back to bite you. If your budget is too big you might scare off a potential sponsor. On the other hand, if your budget is not in line with your production ideas a potential sponsor may feel you are too inexperienced or unrealistic. There are budget templates and budget software programs out there to help you create a budget but most beginning filmmakers need to consult with a professional who knows the ends and outs of breaking down a script.

Filmmaker's Statement and Biography

Include a short biographical sketch of each of the principal filmmakers. Describe any film grants that you have won and sponsors that you have secured. Be sure you attach the appropriate documents in an appendix. Include past awards and notable achievements as well. Attach letters of recommendation from industry professionals, letters from key officials supporting your project, and letters of support from industry mentors and advisors.

Eva is available for personal consultations, script revisions, and proposal writting at www.eva@SNAFUfilms.com.

If you need to brush up on your writing skills Eva suggests William Strunk's The Elements of Style, *now available online at* http://www.bartleby.com/, *and Purdue University's online writing lab located at* http://owl.english.purdue.edu/

Both of these resources feature search engines that allow you to easily find answers to your writing and grammar questions. Just remember, if you hire a professional writer to help you with your proposal, make sure your passion is projected in the final proposal.

The most important thing is never give up! Keep applying for those grants and keep your project in front of potential funders.

Even if you're on the right track, you'll get run over if you just sit there.

—*Will Rogers*

LOADING THE BASES

You've polished your proposal and perfected your pitch. Before you step out of the bullpen make sure you understand the rules of the game.

Rule #1: Know the Catcher Before You Pitch

The number one complaint from funders is too many applications do not fit within the foundation's guidelines. Don't try to throw a fastball past a seasoned funder. Carefully read the guidelines and criteria of each potential funding source. If your project doesn't fit don't apply.

Rule #2: Develop a Strategy

You can't invite a bunch of friends over, order pizza and beer and send off a mass mailing of your proposal. It just doesn't work that way. You must have a specific strategy based on each individual funder. To develop this strategy you need to know where each individual funder is coming from. You must know what makes them tick. You must understand their objectives.

Rule #3: Play The Field

Don't make the mistake of focusing all of your efforts on one funder or on one specific type of funding. Keep your options open. Learn everything you can about different financing opportunities that are available to independent filmmakers and romance every appropriate funding source you can find.

Funders want to fund films that are going to be made and distributed. This means they want to know that you are out there trying to secure additional funding.

Rule #4: There's No Crying in Baseball

Don't view rejection as failure; see it as an opportunity to learn and improve. Follow up with each funder. Thank them for their consideration and ask for feedback. If the funder still shows interest in your project, ask if you can reapply in the future. If the funder is not interested in supporting this particular project thank them for their time and keep the lines of communication open; they may be interested in funding future projects.

Remember, even the best grant writers end up with far more rejections than they do grants. If you are not accumulating several rejections a month then you are not pitching hard enough.

Scouting the Majors: Researching Funders

You know your funder is out there floating around somewhere in cyberspace but somehow you just keep missing each other. When you get tired of knocking on the front door maybe it's time to try something different.

Try searching for films that are similar to yours. Find out who funded these films and research these funders. Research documentary film sites, online film and video magazines, and online video distributors.

Watch films and videos that are similar to yours and research the funders listed in the credits. What businesses, individuals, and corporations do the producers thank? You've just found a list of sponsors who fund film projects like yours! Put these sponsors high on your list of potential funders and start researching their web sites.

Find out who funds film organizations. For practice, visit the Hollywood Film Foundation web site at http://www.hff.org and click on the *Sponsors* hyperlink. You've just found a list of funders who are passionate about film! Now, get creative and find more sites like this.

Is your film about a specific cause? Find nonprofit agencies that advance this cause and find out who their sponsors are. You've just found a list of funders who fund your subject! Research these sponsors and see if they fund media or film projects. These are people who might be willing to act as your sponsors or mentors, and may lead you to additional funding opportunities.

You've been surfing the net for years, but are you up on the latest search tools? Do you really know Boolean logic? Do you know how to access information that normal search engines can't reach? Do you know the difference between a spider, a crawler, and a MetaSearcher? If not, take an afternoon and brush up on your surfing skills. UC Berkeley offers an award winning Internet tutorial located at http://www.lib.berkeley.edu/TeachingLib/Guides/Internet.

The Internet has revolutionized the way we access information but please don't forget about your local library. Your library probably has an entire collection devoted to foundations and grants, including some of those expensive databases. Take the time to pay a personal visit to your library and meet the Grants and Foundations Librarian. She can show you valuable trade secrets on how to search different databases and give you pointers on how to find other possible donors for your film. Your local librarian may turn out to be one of the most helpful people on your film crew!

Organizing Your Search

Some people are good at finding information—they're so good they accumulate file cabinets and desk drawers full of computer printouts, newspaper articles, and magazine clippings. You know how it is, you can't get to it today but you may want to read it someday so it's added to the stack of papers precariously perched on the corner of your desk. This is not information, it's clutter!

Anything unfinished, unused, unresolved, or disorganized, bogs us down and keeps us from moving forward. You will need to keep a list of potential funders so you can keep track of your funding contacts, but please don't let the list get away from you. It's tempting to start compiling a giant list of potential funders for future projects but try to keep your eyes on your current goal. The key to being a successful researcher is not to accumulate piles of information that you may need someday, but to know how to find the information you need when you need it.

There are all kinds of complicated databases and fancy tracking systems designed to organize your business contacts; however, your objective is to get your film made, not learn how to use some complicated color-coded filing system, or the latest software program. A simple list is all you need. It should include the funder's name, address, their web and e-mail address; contact person; and a place for notes.

*We gain strength, and courage, and confidence by each
experience in which we really stop to look fear in the
face . . . we must do that which we think we cannot.*
—*Eleanor Roosevelt*

FOUNDATIONS AND GRANTS

A foundation is a nonprofit organization that donates
(or grants) money, equipment or other supplies to organizations and individuals. Foundations are also called charitable trusts, endowments, and public charities.

Private foundations are usually funded from one source,
typically an individual, a family, or a corporation, while
public foundations are built from multiple sources, including grants from private foundations, government agencies,
and donations from private individuals. Foundations have
a responsibility to uphold the principles of the foundation
and make sure their funder's donations are being used for
the intended purpose.

If you've searched for funding in the past you already
know that many foundations will not grant money to individuals. Will these foundations make an exception? Sometimes, but it's rare. Donating funds to an individual is complicated because the IRS requires nonprofits to obtain advance approval before distributing funds to individuals.

So, what's a starving artist to do? One option is to find a
fiscal sponsor.

Fiscal Sponsorship

Another important step in the *Art of Funding Your Film* is to investigate the possibility of using a fiscal agent for your project.

Fiscal Sponsors receive and administer funds and provide various levels of organizational support to individuals. In short, a fiscal sponsorship can give you access to funding opportunities and other resources available to 501(c)(3) non-profit organizations! Private individuals will also be more likely to donate their hard earned money if you have fiscal sponsorship because they can use the donation as a tax write-off.

Remember, a fiscal sponsorship is a relationship and like all relationships it is important to find the right match. Each fiscal sponsor has different guidelines and goals. Some fiscal agents charge a fee or commission; others are simply altruistic spirits who are dedicated to your cause. Just make sure you and your fiscal sponsor have a clear agreement regarding the management and disbursement of funds, what fees, if any, the fiscal agent will charge, and who will retain legal identity and control over your project.

Schools, arts organizations, or other local community groups often sponsor individual filmmakers. *New York Foundation for the Arts* (www.nyfa.org) posts a list of fiscal sponsors that are located all over the country.

Finding the Grantor to Match Your Film

The money to make your film is out there. Foundations have money and resources already set aside to give away to the right individual or organization. It's their job to give these resources away. Your job is to make sure your project matches their criteria and guidelines.

Choose a potential funder from the list in Appendix H and visit their website. Start with their mission statement, then go directly to their funding guidelines. When you find a funder that looks promising, dig in and explore their web site from top to bottom. Learn everything you can about this funding source. When was the foundation established? Who established it and why? Find out who funds the foundation. As you research, jot down questions that come to mind.

If you've gotten this far and the foundation still feels like a good match dig a little deeper. What causes have they funded in the past? You're probably not going to want to pitch your documentary about endangered marmots of the San Juan Wilderness to an organization that is an ardent supporter of the *Independent Taxidermists of America.* Knowing what type of organizations or individuals a particular funding source has embraced in the past will give you additional insight into the types of projects they fund.

IRS 501(c)(3) defines nonprofit, charitable, tax-exempt organizations. IRS Form 990 is used by tax-exempt organizations, nonexempt charitable trusts, and political organizations to provide the IRS with information required by section 6033. *Why should you care?* Because you can find out a lot about an organization by accessing their tax forms.

I know, it sounds positively sneaky, doesn't it? Don't worry, I'm not asking you to put on a cat suit and slip into their business office at night with a flashlight. These records are available to the public. If you're into snooping (and what great filmmaker isn't?) then you'll want to stay awake for this next part.

Form 990 discloses all kinds of juicy tidbits about an organization's finances, board members, and, you guessed it, their philanthropic activities. Accessing this one form will tell you what kind of programs the organization supports and the names of all grant recipients for that fiscal year. It will also give you the name, address, and phone number of the operations officer (the person in charge of the grant you are applying for), and whether or not they accept unsolicited proposals.

You can access information on over 70,000 U.S. private and community foundations for free through the Foundation Center's *Foundation Finder*, located at www.fdncenter.org. If you don't have the name of a foundation, GrantSmart (http://www.grantsmart.org) offers a database of U.S. grantmakers and foundations you can search using keywords.

Give it a try! Access the Foundation Finder and type in "Internet Science Education Project," and you will be given direct access to a PDF link containing this foundation's most current individual tax records. Here you will learn that the *Internet Science Education Project* supports the advancement of time travel to the past. Cool!

Part I, 25 on Page 1 of their Form 990 tells you they donated $321,215 in contributions, gifts and grants during the 2001 fiscal year. Zip on over to Part VIII, 1, and you will find the name of their president and discover that he was paid $108,210 for this dubious distinction. Part IX-(A) gives you a summary of their four largest direct charitable activities, which included donations for the research and development of "nanotechnology and the advanced propulsion of space craft."

Beam on over to Part XV, 3, and you will find a list of all of the grants and contributions *ISEP* paid during the fiscal year as well as a list of grants and contributions they have approved for future funding.

You may not be the least bit interested in a foundation that funds nanotechnology or space travel, but it doesn't take a rocket scientist (sorry) to see how this one little tax form can provide a wealth of information about a foundation that you *are* interested in. *The Foundation Center* has a very slick diagram of a 990-PF that shows you exactly where the most important funding information is located. You can download it for free at http://fdncenter.org/funders/990pffly.pdf.

Find a potential funding source for your film project and check out the operations officer. Who's on the Board? Who won last year's grant competition? How about the year before? Try to find web sites of past winners and learn every-thing you can about their projects. E-mail them and con-gratulate them on their award and say something positive about their film. Tell them you are applying for the same grant and ask them if they have any suggestions, tips, or advice. Remember, jot down questions as they come to you; you will need them later.

A grant can be a stepping-stone for a first time film-maker who is trying to break into the industry. Barbara Liebowitz had never made a film before when she won her *Roy W. Dean Grant* and she has since gone on to make docu-mentaries for major cable companies. There are other foun-dations out there that will take a chance on an emerging filmmaker if the project and the filmmaker match the foundation's philosophy. If you are a first time filmmaker make sure the grant you are applying for supports emerg-ing filmmakers. Perhaps you can increase your chances if you attach an experienced crew to your project. Checkout the qualifications and past experience of previous grant winners and research their film crew.

The next step in *The Art of Funding Your Film* is to find a foundation that looks promising—this is the part you've been waiting for!

Take out your list of questions and choose the best one. You are going to call the person who funds the grant. Place your call between 10 A.M. and 12 P.M., or between 2 P.M. and 4 P.M. and ask to speak directly with the operations officer in charge of the grant. If they don't answer try again later. If you must, leave your name and number and the best time you can be reached, then make sure you're ready when they call back. If you leave your cell phone number, keep your cell phone turned on and be ready with pen and paper handy.

Don't worry, they will call you; it's their job. You did your homework. You know what the foundation is about and you know they support projects like yours, so they will

71

be interested in what you have to say. Individuals who work for nonprofits are passionate about their cause. They are overworked and underpaid. They believe the world needs more films on important issues and they want to help you get your film made.

So what are you going to say when you get them on the phone? Remember that pitch you've been working on? You are going to tell them who you are and give them the concept of your film using that stunning two-paragraph pitch that you have worked so hard on. Write it down and keep it with you so you are ready when the phone rings. You know your pitch by heart. I know this and you know this, but you just might be a tad nervous so believe me, write it down. Your initial approach is critical so let's go over the steps:

- You have the name of the person, the correct spelling and pronunciation.
- You have read this person's bio and you know about their past contributions. Compliment them and thank them for their continuing efforts to independent filmmakers.
- You have read the web site thoroughly and you know what type of projects they fund.
- You have an important question to ask.
- You have your pitch in front of you.
- You're organized.
- You will not keep them on the phone long.
- You have researched prior winners and you know that your film fits within the scope of previously funded projects.

Get ready to take some notes!

I love it when filmmakers ask questions. Sometimes they ask how many applications we receive, or how many grants we fund per year. These are important questions. I can hear them doing the math in their heads as they try to determine what their chances are.

Most filmmakers will pitch their project then pause and wait for my response. This is good because it allows me time to process what they have just said. I usually reply with a question. They will typically have a quick answer that will lead to another question. This is what you want to achieve with this first call. You want to spark interest and draw the funder into the heart of your project.

Do not keep the funder on the phone too long, and do not over-pitch your film. Take a breath between sentences and allow the funder adequate time to respond. We know you are passionate about your film but learn to listen to feedback and remember to come up for air!

Once in a while I'll get some eager filmmaker on the line who sounds like he's flying on his third or fourth Starbucks. Information is coming in so fast and furious that I don't know what's hit me! I don't have time to ask questions because he never stops. When he finally pauses long enough to take a breath, I find that I've lost most of my questions, then just when I start to regain my balance he'll start up again. All I can do is wait until he runs out of steam.

> *I would have talked less and listened more if I had my life to live over.*
> —*Erma Bombeck*

Listening is an art. My father, Roy W. Dean, was a wonderful listener. When dad retired I asked him to move to Southern California and help me run *Studio Film and Tape*. I opened shop in 1968, and started selling short-ends*. I noticed that there was always a lot of leftover film at the end of each feature film production and thought if I could get access to all this unused film I could recycle it and sell it. I ignored all the skeptics, put on my mini-skirt and boots, marched over to Universal Studios and asked them for "those little ol' short ends that you really don't want."

*Carole coined the term "short-ends," which is now a standard industry phrase. Her business, *Studio Film and Tape* quickly grew into a multimillion-dollar business.

Before long I was buying up short-ends all over Hollywood, testing them and selling them for a profit.

I was thrilled when dad sold his house in Dallas and moved to California in mid-life to start over again with me. He could have had any job in the office, but he chose to work at the front counter because he wanted to meet the filmmakers as they came in to buy film and sound stock. Dad never grew tired of listening to filmmakers describe their latest projects. He would literally end up spending hours with one filmmaker because he would ask the magic question that every filmmaker loves to hear: "So tell me, what are you shooting these days?"

Renee Ross and I got pretty good at anticipating the magic question. Dad would be up there at his post chatting away with some new filmmaker while Renee and I were busy working behind the scenes. Suddenly we could sense that it was coming. He was going to ask! Renee and I would stop, look at each other then we would start waving our arms, trying to get dad's attention. We'd shake our heads and mouth, "No! No!"

But it never did any good. Every time a new filmmaker came through the front door Renee and I knew that dad was going to ask that magic question. We could be scrambling around, waiting on customers, pulling our hair out, and dad would be up there at the counter listening intently as some filmmaker described his latest masterpiece.

I always try to remember dad's patience when I have a "Starbucker" on the phone. Sometimes I will go outside, water my plants, prune my roses, come back in and fix a cup of hot tea while the filmmaker goes on like an Animaniac on crack.

Often when people go on like this it is because they are nervous. Calm yourself. Don't feel as though you need to fill every moment of silence with some profound statement. Develop the art of listening. When you let funders participate in the conversation they will be able to process what you are saying. They will formulate questions and will ulti-mately remember more about you and your project.

Okay, back to your phone call. After you have delivered your perfect one-paragraph pitch, ask the funder if your project fits their criteria then listen. Remember, your phone call serves two purposes: you are trying to find out if the funder will accept a proposal for the film you want to make, and you want to create a connection with this person. This is probably the first person that will read your application; it may be the *only* person who reads your application, so leave a good impression.

Funders will often ask questions to determine whether or not a particular project fits their foundation's criteria. Don't worry if you can't answer every question. You are still in preproduction and have not made a decision regarding a particular question, so just explain this to them and move on. Above all, listen to what they have to say. Stay awake, take notes, and pick up all the clues you can.

If you find out that you have made a production deci-sion that will disqualify your project consider changing di-rections. When you play the funding game you must un-derstand that you may have to include or exclude specific criteria in order to get funding from a particular organiza-tion. Believe me, there are worse things in life, so consider it. What you want to do is maintain control of the film and most of these grants can help you do that.

What do you say if the funder tells you that your film does *not* fit the foundation's criteria? Thank her for her time, offer some sincere words of gratitude for the job she is do-ing, and let her know you will contact her again when you have something that fits their criteria. Then go out and buy a nice Hallmark card and write a personal note thanking her once again for listening to your pitch. Remind her of the title of your film, and send along your best wishes for the future success of the foundation. If she gives you the thumbs up, thank her for her time and confirm her address (oh, and please wait until you hang up to let out that scream). Go out and pick up a nice Hallmark card and write a brief note inside thanking her for the time she spent discussing your film about the endangered marmots of the San Juan Wilderness. Include a condensed version of your pitch and let her know that you will be applying for the grant. Sign your name and post it with a colorful endangered species postage stamp.

Why send her a card? Because film funders talk to each other. If you become a grant finalist with another foundation she will probably either hear about it or read about it. She will remember your card and think about you and your project in a good light.

You have now made two connections with the woman who will be handling your first application. Make a note on your list of potential funders and call her back in six to eight weeks with another important question. Send her a card for every occasion from *Independence Day* to *National Marmot Day*. Include a brief note about your film along with your condensed pitch and wish her a happy holiday.

Keep each potential funder close to your project by keeping them up to date on your progress and achievements. Let potential funders know if you win another grant, or if you have found an award-winning director for your project. When Albert Maysles agrees to be your mentor, send your potential funder an update. Remember to keep track of each contact that you make. When you keep your funders involved in your progress they will be drawn deeper and deeper into your project. When your application crosses their desk they will remember you and your film. I know this from experience.

JanEva Hornbaker was a finalist for my Roy W. Dean L.A. Film Grant, and was applying for our New York grant for her documentary, *Searcher for Souls*. Eva's film follows modern-day explorers who search for the remains of more than 78,000 Americans still missing from the Second World

War. Eva had the most fantastic adventures while she was in Europe researching her film, and she took the time to share each dramatic event with me. I felt as though I was right there with her through it all as I received e-mail after e-mail from exotic locations in the south of France and southern Italy. She told me about her special press conference with the mayor of Cannes; the rainy afternoon in southern France when she discovered the whereabouts of a lost American Flyer; and her phone call from the Pentagon. With each e-mail I grew closer to Eva and her project.

There is something special that happens when a funder picks up an application from a filmmaker who has kept her close to the project. Once a funder has been swept into your passion she is inwardly cheering for you. She is already connected to you and your film.

Keep all of your notes organized and continue to look for questions that you can ask. When the next month rolls around, pick up the phone and make your second call. Reintroduce yourself and your project and ask another question that is not already answered on the website. Get the answer, take notes, thank her, and let her get back to work.

In six weeks, call back and introduce yourself and your project once again, ask another important, unanswered question. Take notes, thank her, and let her get back to work. As you work on your proposal you will generate more questions and so it is natural to keep in touch this way.

Decide how many organizations you will research each day then make a commitment to sit down and put in your quota every day. Give up those Seinfeld and Friends reruns and use that time to search the Web. Filmmakers often go back and use the same funders for subsequent projects. Just know that while your initial search may be time consuming, it can also lead to future funding.

Work your way through the list of funders included in this book. As you work, add funders you find along the way. You will have to kiss a lot of frogs to find a prince (or princess), but once you've found one it's worth it.

Carole Dean awarding Paul Davidson the New
Zealand film grant for "Giving it all away"!

RAISING FUNDS FROM INDIVIDUALS AND BUSINESSES

I have a confession to make. When I was running *Studio Film* I used to hide in a corner office so filmmakers couldn't find me. Of course my wonderful dad (who was powerless to a filmmaker's passionate pitch) would give me up every single time!

Small businesses and corporations are untapped goldmines for independent filmmakers. Local businesses and corporations always have managers (or dads) who are very accessible and easy to talk to. Be it my dad, or one of my employees, someone was always knocking on my door in the middle of the day with some filmmaker's proposal. It was usually only a one-page proposal, which was a blessing since business seemed to grind to a halt whenever this occurred. Customers could be lined up at the counter but it didn't matter. Everyone in the office got wrapped up in the drama that was unfolding. You could practically hear the drum roll in the background. Would she say yes or no?

Looking back now I realize this was probably a conspiracy since everyone knew the buck stopped with me. People everywhere (yes, even people in Hollywood) want to be involved in a film.

When I scanned these proposals I would look for the following things:

- The story synopsis (hopefully brief and to the point).
- Why the filmmaker was making the film.
- Exactly what the filmmaker needed and why.
- Who would benefit from the film.

- What the filmmaker was willing to do for me (an end-credit, product placement, etc.).
- How much the donation would mean to the filmmaker.

If you have a fiscal sponsor, make sure to note this on all of your proposals. Your tax-deductible status will go a long way when looking for donations. Customize your proposal for each individual business you approach. When you make it personal the recipient feels special.

Start by making a list of all the stores and restaurants near your location. Visit the managers of these businesses with your one page customized proposal in your hand and the best smile you can muster. Don't forget to dress the part. Wear a *Kodak Film* cap and have a *Maxell* bag slung around your shoulder. Make sure they see *you* and think *Spielberg.*

Sometimes you have to leave your proposal with an employee. Pitch the employee the same way you would the manager. Be considerate to all of the employees. If they are anything like the wonderful people who worked with me at *Studio Film,* once they get caught up in your enthusiasm they are going to beg their manager to become involved in your film. Think of the employees as your support team. Mention how much your crew enjoys their pizza, or how impressed you were the last time they did some copy work for you. Talk about your film and give your pitch as though you are asking for a $10,000 grant.

Most managers can make the decision right there on the spot without going to a corporate supervisor. I did business at *Kinko's* for years before I asked who I could see about getting a discount. When the woman at the counter told me she could help me I was flabbergasted. I thought I would need to fill out reams of forms that would be sent off through the chain of command. All I had to do was explain that I represented a nonprofit organization that helped filmmakers and ask for a discount. It was that easy!

Most independents forget that all of the little miscellaneous budget items add up. You are going to be into *Kinko's* for about $800 and *Office Depot* for another $1200. The caterer is going to hit you up for about $2500 for lunches, and you are probably going to have to fork over about $800 a week for equipment rental. All of these little extras can easily add another $6000-$10,000 to your bottom line.

Go through your shooting script and your budget and make a list of all the things that might be donated through local businesses and corporations. Are you going to need a rental car? What about office supplies? You know you're going to have to feed your crew and your new cameraman can put away three pizzas in one sitting! Your list might include car rental agencies, grocery stores, bagel shops, the local pizza parlor. List any business that advertises. Targeting small businesses like the little mom and pop coffee shop around the corner is often more productive than going to a large corporate business like *Starbucks*. Local business people want to support their community and they will be receptive to your needs. A business in a bustling neighborhood may have a lot of healthy competition. If this is the case, mention the discount offered by their competitor and ask if they can beat it.

The most popular labor-saving device is still money.
—Phyllis George

If you can't get it for free, do your homework and know what you can get it for. Dov S-S Simons of *HollywoodU.com* says you can get a discount on everything in your production budget. According to Dov, "no one who knows anything in the industry pays the rate card price." Know what the going rate card is and ask for a discount.

Studio Film's three-tier price index was installed on every employee's computer. Businesses do this. Every salesperson knows the lowest price they can quote. This is the rate you want, even if you just buy ten items. Once your name is linked in the computer with a special rate you will get that rate every time you make a purchase. I have made special arrangements with David Cohen of *Edgewise*. Film-makers who enter my *Roy W. Dean* grants will receive a discount for all of *Edgewise's* products, including film, tape, and digital supplies. If you apply for my grant and you would like to receive this discount, call Hank at 800-824-3130 and he will get you in the computer as a *Roy W. Dean* grant applicant.

Bobby Mardis (one of my favorite producers) once told me that he never takes anything personal when he is pro-ducing a film. He gets the local production book, goes down it from A to Z, and starts asking. He explains how much he can spend and what he needs. If a business manager can't accommodate him he thanks her, tells her he will try her again on a future production, then he moves down the list and tries the next vendor. He keeps at it until he finds some-one who will give him what he needs at the price he has budgeted.

When you contact *Kinko's, Jim's Car Rentals,* or the lo-cal bagel shop, begin by asking for a donation in exchange for a mention in your film's credits or for product place-ment. If they can't accommodate you and they are the only game in town, ask them if they would be willing to give you a 25% discount if you promote their business to the cast and crew. Always ask for a donation first and save the re-quest for a discounted price as your last resort.

Remember, most companies work on a 25-40% profit so when you ask for a 25% discount you are asking the com-pany to donate most of their profits to the film. Let them put a sign in the lobby that mentions they are donating to your film. Tell them you will pose for pictures, or let them shoot pictures of the cast and crew during production to use in an ad for the local paper. Turn it into a great PR opportunity for them. Sometimes just offering to give a local businessperson a copy of the finished videotape is all it takes to get a smile and a donation.

Once you go over your budget carefully and list all the printing, copying, beverages, food, cell phones, cars, airline tickets, restaurant charges, and so on, you will be amazed at how much money you can save by finding resources through local businesses.

You can also negotiate with your crew. Many producers look for a production assistant who has a truck or an RUV then they negotiate a flat weekly salary that includes the use of their vehicle. Your P.A. should be one of your first employees as they can free you from time-consuming jobs, like local pickup and deliveries. They can even do your shopping, get the cleaning, or walk the dog. Your P.A. can do those time consuming jobs that take you away from the focus of your film, while you work on the art of funding your film!

Producing 140 shows, working with countless filmmakers over the last 33 years, and raising close to $2 million in goods and services for my *Roy W. Dean Film Grants*, has taught me some valuable lessons. Never forget that the film business is a business. Before you approach a business or an individual, make a list of all of the benefits they will receive from your proposed venture. If their benefits do not outweigh your benefits then you need to rethink your proposal. Your contacts will be more responsive when they know you are concerned with their image and their profits.

RAISING FUNDS FROM INDIVIDUALS

In *The United Arts Funds* report for fiscal year 2001, a profile of support patterns for nonprofit arts organizations shows individuals (you know, those people that live in your hometown) are the largest contributors to overall revenues for the arts. [v]

When filmmakers approach individuals, they are looking for either an investor or a donor. It is essential that you disclose exactly what you are looking for and that you are completely honest when you discuss your film's investment potential.

Have a good attorney on board before you approach an individual investor. Do not take one dime from an investor until you have presented the investor with an investment memorandum. Mark Litwak discusses the legal side the producer/investor relationship later on in the chapter on Financing Independent Films. It is essential that you heed Mark's words. There are laws that protect investors and these laws are very clear.

Contributions do not require paperwork. Just send your donor a letter of thanks and the information they need for their taxes and you're on your way to the bank! Of course approaching an individual donor will require a serious investment of your time. Please do not approach your family and friends and immediately ask them to donate toward your film. Remember, when you ask someone to donate or invest in your film they are essentially investing in you.

Romancing individual funders requires as much skill as creating a great pitch or writing a strong proposal. You must sharpen your people skills and be prepared to spend some serious time dodging the moths that fly out their purses. "Doing time" sound like a line from *The Sopranos*, but that's exactly what it takes. You need to put time into building a relationship with any potential donor.

If you met someone at a party and proposed marriage over cocktails they would think you were crazy! You have to win their interest, their trust, and their confidence first. Potential donors need to know you and they need to know your film. They need to know why this film has to be made and why you are the only one who can make it. They need to see how dedicated you are to the project. Get them interested in your film before you ever ask them for a thing. Invite them to production meetings, script sessions, and fundraising parties.

A filmmaker told me a wonderful story about a wealthy donor he was courting. The donor told the filmmaker that her husband had taken a small business and turned it into a multimillion-dollar corporation. She told the story with great pride, and it was obvious that she loved and admired her husband very much, so the filmmaker asked her if he could film an interview with her husband. He taped the interview, did a little editing, and presented her with an hour of her husband's life story. She immediately attached herself to the filmmaker because the filmmaker knew what was important to her. Do you think he got his donation? Of course he did! But he built a relationship with her before he even thought about asking.

So, where do you find these wealthy philanthropists? Remember those old address books you stored in your closet after you bought your palm pilot? Dust them off and start looking for names. Find people in there who could easily part with five grand or more and not miss it. You might be surprised at how many names you come up with. As the years go by people move up the ladder so don't discount someone who was a sales manager back in 1993. She might be the head of the company today. I don't care if you haven't talked to her in years. Pull out that name, make that phone call and tell her about the film you're making.

Reestablish your relationship. Tell her you are producing a film about very important issue and you thought she would enjoy hearing about it. Perhaps she has good business sense. Ask her for some advice, but don't mention money. People will donate time to help you when they see that you are on an important quest. Get her involved then send her a one or two page proposal. Call her up and invite her to a production meeting or a fundraising party.

She may suspect that you are going to pop the money question and she may turn you down. That's okay; you just saved yourself some time. Other contacts will take you up on your offer, especially if you have asked for advice in their area of expertise. The key is, you must *get to know* these people. You must understand who they are and what their needs are before you can ask for money.

Take some time and brainstorm. Think about people you have worked for over the past ten years. What about your spouse's affiliations? Do you know someone who donates time to a public official? If so, ask if you can get an introduction. It may take weeks for you to come up with a list but that's okay. Fundraising is an important part of the art of funding your film. Most of the producers you meet in Hollywood will tell you that they have several projects in various stages of production, which is a dead giveaway that they are out there looking for money.

If you are doing a film about a woman who has survived cancer, seek funding from cancer survivors, from family members of cancer victims, and from nonprofit cancer organizations. If you are doing a film about the plight of our oceans whose name comes to mind? How about Ted Danson and the American Oceans Campaign? Contact Mr. Danson, tell him about your project and ask him for some advice. Go to the American Oceans Campaign web site and research their sponsors. Remember Form 990 from Chapter 5, *Foundations & Grants*? This form also lists individuals who have donated to the foundation.

How do you get to know potential donors once you have found them? It may be as simple as picking up the phone and calling them. Give them your two-paragraph pitch but don't ask for money. Tell them that you are researching your subject and ask them about their organization. Look for people who can help you with information on your subject matter.

Concerned citizens who have money usually know other concerned citizens who have money. Take the time to get to know each individual and listen to what they have to say about your subject. Once you have established a relationship, find a role for this person somewhere on your project.

Perhaps they could help throw a fundraising party, be the expert advisor on your subject, or act as your mentor. Investors and donors will pay special attention to your proposal if you have people like this on board.

You must be persistent. When I first started out in the film business skeptics told me that no one in their right mind would buy short-ends. I had to overcome some heavy opposition to get going, but I was determined. Capturing a market is like fishing with a net. If you work one market at a time it is much easier to capture the entire market when you land your first sale within that market.

I started out by making cold calls to film schools. I had to keep at it for over a month before I got my first order, but as soon as I took that order I hung up and called the film school down the road and told them their competitor just placed an order. Suddenly they were interested. My cold call sales ratio went from a 5% return to a 30% return because I was working within a tight industry where people know each other. I stayed with my idea of selling to one market (film schools) until I captured one fish in that market. Businesses and corporations are more open to a new idea when they discover their peers are interested in the idea.

Consider doing the same thing when you look for individuals to fund your film. If Mary Smith from *Americans for Cleaner Oceans* has agreed to act as your mentor, go to similar organizations within the community and make a list of their board members. Call each person and develop a relationship. Let them know that Mary Smith from *Americans for Cleaner Oceans* is working with you. These methods will provide you with advisors, mentors, and donors.

What if you can't get them on the phone? What if your potential donor is as reclusive as Howard Hughes? Get to know his secretary or his personal assistant. This is how good sales people become successful sales people. Secretaries and personal assistants can get you through to the people you want to know, so take some time and create a rapport with these people. Get on a first name basis with a potential donor's secretary. Chat with her about her vacation. Ask her about her children. If you are professional and personable, and if you have a good pitch, you will get through to the person you want. A secretary's job is to protect her boss. If she believes that you will not embarrass her, and that you have something important to present, she will put your call through.

It's all in your approach. Sherrie Findhorn was one of my top sales people. Before Sherrie came to *Studio Film* she worked for the *Yellow Pages*. This is where she learned to smile on the phone. That's right, Sherrie told me that sales shot up when some executive put mirrors on every sales person's desk and asked them to smile when they made their cold calls. Try it! Especially on a day when you feel like biting the heads off nails. You will be treated better and it will lift your spirits.

Don't be afraid to go to the top of the ladder. I know these people are often hard to get to but that just makes success that much sweeter! Who do you think wrote my first ad for *Studio Film and Tape NYC* back in 1970? The late Ira Eaker, cofounder of Back Stage! The first time I went to see Ira he asked to see my copy. I was so green back in those days I didn't even know what a copy was, but Ira took the time to work out a great ad for me. I ran that ad for years. Ira and I remained good friends right up to his recent death. Sometimes the nicest people are at the top. They may be hidden away by a protective secretary but if you believe in your project you can find a way in.

"Okay Carole, so when do I get to ask the $64,000 question?" Be patient grasshopper. Don't even think about asking for money until you have all your preproduction ducks in a row. Form your production company and put together a solid preproduction package while you're getting close to these potential donors and investors.

Popping the Big Question

You have put together a strong preproduction package and you have taken the time to establish a good relationship with your donor. You know what they are looking for and you feel confident that your project is a good fit.

Now you are ready to ask!

Sit down with them in their living room, or take them out to a nice restaurant, look them right in the eye and ask them if they will donate to your project. Say something like, "would you be willing to donate $10,000 to my film?"

They have heard your pitch so many times they know it by heart so don't pitch them again. Instead, give them a production update. Tell them about some of the grants you have applied for and talk about where you expect to get the rest of your financing. Be one-hundred percent honest in every statement that you make.

They know all about the paperwork inside that preproduction package lying next to you on the table. You have discussed many of these things with them over the past year and they have given you advice along the way. Perhaps they even helped you with some of the paperwork inside that package. Don't remind them that you have a nonprofit fiscal sponsor and that their donation will be tax deductible. They know that. This is not a *why don't you look it over and let me know later* meeting, this is a look *me in the eye and give me an answer* meeting.

Remember, you are asking this person to invest in you. You already know they trust and respect you. You know they want to help you complete your film. You have invested a great deal of time to bring this person into your film and you would not be sitting across from them now if they did not have the same passion for your project that you have. Your chances of walking away with a check are going to be ten thousand times better than if you had just sent them a package in the mail and followed up with a phone call.

How much are you going to ask for? If you ask for too much you will probably walk away empty handed. Most donors do not like to admit that they can't afford to donate $70,000, but they might be able to swing $10,000. Do your homework and know how much they have donated in the past to causes like yours and make sure you approach them with a figure they can afford. Don't embarrass them by asking for too little—that's even worse than asking for too much!

If you want to make that film, set a deadline and start working. I know that you work on your grant application right up to the deadline then *Fed-Ex* it overnight because I'm the one that gets bombarded with a ton of applications the day before the deadline! Filmmakers always work best under pressure. Barbara Trent told me that she always used to get her grant applications in just under the wire. One of the grants Barbara tried to win finally eliminated their deadline policy and opened the door for submissions anytime during the calendar year. Barbara said she never applied for the grant again. We need deadlines, so set one and start getting results.

I want you to open your mind to all of the creative ways to raise money. The money is out there. You just have to approach fundraising with the same level of creativity that you use throughout the entire filmmaking process. Think of fundraising as another art form.

Your Fundraising Toolbox

The 10-minute promo

A ten-minute promotional tape is one of the most valuable resources you can have in your fundraising toolbox. When Barbara Liebowitz won the Roy W. Dean film grant for her film, *Salvaged Lives*, she showed up at my office at seven o'clock the next morning ready to shoot. Less than a month later Barbara presented her uncut footage to the East Coast IFP where she secured more financing. Film is a visual medium and it's hard to sell this kind of product on paper. Creating a 5 to 10 minute promo tape is one of your most important goals in the art of funding your film.

Win a grant

Barbara knew winning the Roy W. Dean Film Grant would provide her with the equipment and professional services that would help her get started. Look for grants like this so you can get out there and start shooting. Winning a grant is like priming the pump; it will empower you as a filmmaker and start the ball rolling for more funds and donations. Potential investors and donors are more likely to fund a filmmaker who has already won a grant. Use the name of the donor on all of your grant applications and hire a public relations person to get the most you can from this first win.

P-a-r-t-y!

In The Fundraising Houseparty, author Morrie Warshawski tells filmmakers to find a wealthy supporter who shares their cause, then ask them if they would be willing to throw a fundraising party. If you find someone who is well connected they are going to have an amazing house and an amazing guest list. Think about it. They will invite friends and associates who can write a $500 or $5000 check without batting an eye! Pick up a copy of Morrie's book, he has perfected the fundraising houseparty down to the last detail, even the invitations.

Shoot Your Donors!

During your fundraising party have several experienced camera people with digital cameras roam the room and conduct short interviews with possible donors. Edit it on your home computer and produce a short video that addresses your film's cause while highlighting these featured interviews. Offer a copy to guests for a $100 donation. Follow up with everyone who purchased a copy and ask them if they would like to do a more formal interview in exchange for a tax-deductible donation.

I interviewed my dad using an old VHS camera. He told wonderful stories about playing in watermelon patches in Dallas and how the boys would drop a ripe melon on the ground then dig their hands into it enjoying ever last bite. These tapes are priceless and I wouldn't trade them for the world. Think of ways to sell the concept of doing a family interview. It is a marvelous way to leave something for the grandchildren. You can set your own prices. You might charge $3000 for an hour, $2000 for 30 minutes. You are a professional film producer and you will be using the latest equipment and techniques. Just be willing to film a few minions to raise the money it will take for you to start filming the real thing.

Give 'em Credit!

Have you ever noticed that some films seem to have more producers than cast? Producer credits are like money in the bank. An executive producer credit can be worth $50,000, while an associate producer might bring in $20,000. The numbers are based on your budget and the sky's the limit. Be creative and make up a title!

The next time you watch a film sit through the credits. When you come to the part that says, "The Producers wish to thank . . ." read the names and start adding. Each one of those names can be worth $1000 or more. A full screen credit could be worth $5,000. A dedication to the memory of a sponsor's loved one could bring in $10,000 or more.

Finding and developing relationships with funders is hard work but take heart. The hardest part is going after your first funder. Once you get that out of the way you will build your portfolio of funders and other funders will follow. Before long you will create your own network of funding sources. Remember, if you are honest and professional it will be a positive experience and your funders will be there for future projects.

COWBOY ECONOMICS AND ENTREPRENEURS

by Patric Hedlund

Author, *A Bread Crumb Trail through the PBS Jungle: The Producer's Survival Guide see*
http://www.forests.com/breadcrumb

The following was written and edited by Patric Hedlund.

While civilized lands look with horror upon America's passion for cowboy economics and cringe at legislators who label public support for cultural arts as unpatriotic, successful independent producers in the United States often make the discovery that *The Art of Funding Your Film* must quickly evolve into *The Art of Becoming an Entrepreneur.*

Webster's defines an entrepreneur as a person who organizes and manages an enterprise with considerable initiative and risk. Does this have a familiar ring to it? Talent, initiative, sheer guts and dumb luck in the face of risk describe the independent filmmaker. How fortunate the same traits prepare us to be brilliant entrepreneurs? After all, your efforts as a documentary sharpshooter to create a wonderful film deserve to earn a fair market return rather than financial crash-and-burn.

My goal in this chapter is to share some observations about the environment in which we are working as independents today, illustrating a thought process you might find useful when considering a new project. No matter whether you are a profit or nonprofit production company, your financial goals are basically those of every normal American willing to work 20 hours a day for something they care about passionately: 1) to pay yourself for your work; 2) to avoid maxing out your credit cards; 3) to pay back your relatives; 4) to resist the temptation to hawk your grandmother's wedding ring; and 5) to see this film earn enough to boost you forward into financing your next film.

A PERFECT STORM

Unfortunately, the environment of distribution and funding is changing very rapidly. Even Lewis & Clark would have had a tough time mapping the territory that independent producers must navigate today. Changes in technology, government regulations, ownership consolidation, market demand and contract practices are defining new conditions even as you are reading these words. This is exciting. It is also challenging, because no one can offer you a secret vest-pocket oracle to provide the right answers. You have to learn as much as you can about the underlying issues at play today, then define your own goals and be willing to think on your feet. Networking and exchanging information with your peers and colleagues will help greatly. You may also find that you can influence the future by working with organizations trying to level the playing field for independent producers.

THE REAL WORLD

The business model that you start out with may have a far more profound impact on the future of your film than you might expect. Let's consider an illustration. Many independent producers and documentary filmmakers start out with nonprofit public-interest projects.

Let's say you love Three-Spine Sticklebacks--a very amorous fish with fascinating and elaborate courtship rituals. Nothing would make you happier than to apply your brilliant skills as a film producer to the cause of a Three-Spine Stickleback rescue organization. But here's the news blast: if you simply accept money from the Three Spine Stickleback Rescue Team (TSSRT) to produce a film about their worthy work, you may actually find you have doomed your film to very limited broadcast distribution with little or no market value. Your good intentions, the worthiness of the cause, and the fact that the noble TSSRT is a nonprofit organization are irrelevant. This happens.

For instance, not long ago a question came up in a Cinewomen Documentary Group email dialogue on this subject. My answer outlines the kind of thinking process independents may wish to exercise when considering the implications of their business model for a production project. The answer below is based on real-world experience. [For the sake of the questioner's privacy, the details have been slightly altered]

This is the Question:

Q: With a partner, I've been developing an Animal Rescue project for several years for a small non-profit Animal Rescue organization, and it looks like they may be close to getting corporate sponsorship to produce the doc and hire us---finally. Does anyone have experience with contracts between filmmakers and non-profit organizations hiring them to make a documentary?

This is my answer:

A: Congratulations on seeing funding close ahead! I'm a producer and writer, not an attorney, but here are some thoughts that came to mind as soon as I read your note.

Your good news raises issues many of us have to consider. It may be surprising, but basic questions you'll want to ask yourself and your partners are similar to those you would be asking if you were entering an agreement with a for-profit company.

I. Will you be contracting on a WORK-FOR-HIRE basis, in which you relinquish copyright and ownership of the finished product (and all out-take footage) to the nonprofit, expecting to receive only wages?

There are important consequences to consider. The drawback to "Work-for-Hire" for the nonprofit is that this formula may make it difficult for the film to receive broadcast/cable distribution on either commercial or public TV because it will be seen as what it is: a PR package.

Of course the nonprofit may wish to buy broadcast time themselves and distribute it as a sponsored film which they SELF-SYNDICATE. Or they may wish to promote it as a theatrical distribution. If so, is the cost of time-purchases or theatrical promotion and distribution factored into their budget?

II. On the other hand, will you be retaining copyright, and will your company retain rights to all production work-product, ancillaries and outtakes, with sole discretion about secondary uses, including multi-market distribution?

In this case, you might want a LICENSE agreement with the nonprofit, in which you retain ownership of the project but sell (license) to the nonprofit the right to use the film for specified purposes and specified distributions--in return for that license, they pay you a fee.

There is a wonderful thing known as a PRE-LICENSE FEE, which allows you to accept funds prior to production, with agreement on the date when the product is to be delivered for their specified uses. In the past, educational television often offered pre-license fee funding to prime the pump so that diverse noncommercial programming was produced to fulfill the mandate of public television. Perhaps we should encourage public broadcasting to resurrect this custom (see more about surviving negotiations with public television in my book *A Bread Crumb Trail through the PBS Jungle**).

No matter who you make the contract with, be sure to specify how editorial/scripting decisions are to be made. It is important to maintain EDITORIAL AUTONOMY if your film is to be eligible for distribution outside of the nonprofit's closed-circuit uses.

III. Remember that Funding Biases equal Editorial Biases in the eyes of most programmers.

And rightly so. If you truly want to sell broadcast rights to a variety of outlets, you should try to receive additional funding from another source--better still, several other sources--each of which EXCEEDS the amount to be contributed (via license or grant) by your Animal Rescue nonprofit.

This cannot be emphasized enough: To avoid the appearance of editorial bias, the primary funder SHOULD NOT be the subject of the documentary. The mere appearance of bias can be enough to get you disqualified for broadcast consideration by many commercial and noncommercial "public" outlets.

IV. If the third party that wishes to sponsor the film's budget through the nonprofit group is not going to directly benefit from the film's subject, they may reconsider and decide to fund you directly rather than going through the nonprofit group that is featured in your film.

For example, if you have an idea for a film about the dangers of painful toe corns, and the principal sponsor is not *Dr. Scholl's Foot Remedies, Inc.*, but say, *H&R Block Tax Services*, then making a contract between your film company and the funder is one good way to avoid having issues of editorial influence ever being raised by a distributor.

Remember, if tax-deductible 501c3 benefits are of interest to the funder, you can suggest the funds be channeled through a NEUTRAL NONPROFIT FISCAL SPONSOR. There are many to choose from (for instance the International Documentary Association, Women Make Movies, Independent Film Project and many others, including local public television stations).

V. Of course, you may end up with a combination of I and II. You, for instance, could serve as a Work-for-Hire to do a PR package for the Animal Rescue group, but RETAIN EXCLUSIVE RIGHTS TO ALL FOOTAGE AND OUT-TAKES for your company, with a provision in the contract which allows you to make additional versions of the story, maintaining complete editorial autonomy.

All this must be articulated clearly in your written agreement. It may still not be sufficient to persuade many distributors that you are autonomous however, unless the PR package fee is substantially diluted by other funding sources for your final longer film.

VI. In the final analysis, the nonprofit's goals and objectives need to be balanced with what your long term goals and objectives are for your own company.

Please remember that the surest formula for long term viability for an independent production company seem to be that we RETAIN CONTROL OF THE COPYRIGHTS for our own work, with controlling equity shares, Retaining copyright, WITH CONTROL OVER SIGNIFICANT ANCILLARY RIGHTS, will provide an ongoing income source to your company which will help you fund additional films.

Doubtlessly there are many other issues to be considered in settling on a business model, but this is a sample of the kind of dialogue which is valuable to have with your potential production partners and potential distribution outlets BEFORE you decide how to structure the project legally and financially.

I suggest you go through the steps of clarifying your goals, using this outline as a guide, then speak with a qualified intellectual property attorney to make sure the terms of the contract protect both you and the nonprofit adequately. I hope these thoughts are useful.
Sincerely,
Patric Hedlund

NATURE - NURTURE

Erosion of free market opportunity for you as a small business person is something you should be interested in.

Until 1984, broadcasters' public service obligations were taken very seriously. Independent producers were able far more easily to secure support for community interest programming in local and national markets using the "partnership" techniques discussed brilliantly in this book. Such programming served the community and justified the broadcasters' claims that they deserved to retain their valuable license to use the public airwaves.

Under the 1934 Communications Act, the broadcast airwaves are defined as a natural resource belonging to the people of the United States. A two year franchise was licensed to broadcast companies, giving them the right to use an allocated broadcast frequency to make money. In exchange, they were obligated to earn this privilege by providing public service to the community they served. If they failed to serve their communities' needs, the public could file objections to license renewal and the companies could--and did--lose their broadcast licenses.

MACHO MAN: THE EVER-LENGTHENING FRANCHISE LICENSE

Since the 1980's, the broadcasters' lobbyists have succeeded in convincing Washington D.C. to roll back important public interest obligations once supervised by the Federal Communications Commission (FCC). FCC enforcement of public interest obligation has eroded dismally in recent years, and broadcast license periods have crept from two years to eight years in direct correlation with increased campaign contributions by broadcasters, virtually nullifying the effect of community comment on station management. The feedback loop has been broken. Licensees are no longer being held accountable for public service to communities.

THE MIDAS TOUCH

In 1995, network lobbyists succeeded in persuading Washington politicians to let the Financial Interest and Syndication Act expire. Distribution outlets can now produce and own the programming that they air. Of course this distorts the market. Independent producers who bring projects to a market are not negotiating on a level playing field with a network's own competing in-house projects. Even PBS makes calculations about equity ownership values when considering projects, though you will not often hear this admitted. It has been calculated in-house however that PBS' shares in ancillary product sales from children's shows (like plush toys, books, dancing dinosaurs and red puppies) netted enough to subsidize an entire season of prime time *Frontline* in 2001, with change left over.

DOUBLE STANDARDS, DOUBLE BINDS

Without doubt, there is now a double standard in today's broadcast and cable distribution market. When speaking to broadcast networks as an independent producer, you will be asked to play by rules far different from those by which Work-for-Hire projects owned by the distribution channel itself must heed. This is not fair, and it is not the free-market economics which the 1996 Telecommunications Act promised us.

By year 2003, independents find ourselves competing in an entirely new business environment. As this book goes to press, under Chairman Michael Powell, the FCC has rolled back even more rules, allowing even greater consolidation of media ownership, which will allow a single company to own dominant radio, television, cable and newspaper outlets in communities. The implications are obvious. Cross promotion and marketing of network-owned programs, products and political viewpoints will be ubiquitous. There is a strong risk that slanted news coverage will not be vigorously challenged.

Free enterprise and independent voices are stifled when virtual monopoly or oligopoly market pressures are allowed to undercut independent media producers until it is nearly impossible to secure capital or stay in business.

Under such conditions, networks and their contractors can insist on making Work-for-Hire contracts standard, which means that you may be paid for making a film, but you will not own the copyright or any of the ongoing earning power of what you have created. I reported in *A Bread Crumb Trail Through the PBS Jungle* the impact which a similar way of thinking had on independent producers doing business with PBS. Now *Discovery* and other networks are even trying to justify the notion that they not only seize our copyrights, but also abolish the custom of including our production credits on the films we make. The Documentary Credit Coalition has worked brilliantly to hold back this tide, but they need your participation.

LAWS OF PHYSICS AND FREE SPEECH

There is good news on the horizon however. The laws of physics could be on the side of free speech and independent producers.

Digital signals make far more efficient use of the broadcast spectrum than analog signals. Analog waves are so sloppy by comparison, that one of today's analog channels (such as channel 4 or 13) is broad enough to carry FOUR separate digital channels of broadcasting. You can see that if digital transmission gives a 400% expansion of carriage capacity, the license for a single analog channel magically multiplies into the ability to broadcast four digital channels. This means that either license holders have suddenly received a huge windfall at the expense of the U.S. public-- or the public is due a refund of 75% of their broadcast spectrum for use as we see fit.

In 1997 Former FCC Chairman Reid Hundt urged the public to consider what this could mean, but perhaps the public and independent producers were not yet ready to think the issue through.

THE WORLD'S LARGEST TWO-LETTER WORD

The financial implications for independent producers are massive. IF there is political will in Washington, this newly available capacity could be put to wonderful use by education, health delivery, community service, cultural arts groups, nonprofit organizations, new entrepreneurs and independent voices of all kinds.

But history has rarely seen such a large "if." If you wondered why the air-brakes were so suddenly applied to total digital conversion of broadcast channels, it is because the facts outlined above have become obvious to people in the industry you wish to sell your films to. Completing digital conversion may mean loss of control of gigantic windfall profits for the present license holders.

If you have read this far, you may see digital conversion as a great opportunity, especially if you work together with other filmmakers, small business people, nonprofits, unions, guilds, educators and local political representatives to define ways in which reclaimed broadcast spectrum can energize the public service and entrepreneurial small business sectors of our economy that have the deepest impact on the lives of most Americans. Learning the art of funding your film may lead you to help resurrect the open market of ideas in our country. In the meantime, may every fortune cookie you open deliver this message: You are embarking on an adventure in which great frustrations will be balanced by wonderful fun, lasting friendships and worthy service.

Patric Hedlund is a producer and an applied media anthropologist. Her book "A Breadcrumb Trail Through the PBS Jungle: The Independent Producer's Survival Guide" is available at <http://www.forests.com/breadcrumb>. It provides practical guides for independent producers seeking funding and distribution, plus historical background to clarify why business models have recently changed so dramatically. In addition, excerpts from Patric's keynote comments at RealScreen Magazine's summit conference on the funding crisis for documentaries can be found online at her http://www.forests.com site.

. . .Given another shot at life, I would seize every minute...look at it and really see it.... live it...and never give it back. Stop sweating the small stuff.

—Erma Bombeck

FINANCING INDEPENDENT FILMS

Mark Litwak has been a donor for my Roy W. Dean Film and Video Grants for over eight years, and is a great patron of the art of filmmaking. Top filmmakers quote Mark on a daily basis. I sincerely believe Mark's books are a good investment, whether you are new at filmmaking or a seasoned veteran. You will save problems and avoid giving away the store if you have a solid grasp of the legalities of the film industry. Visit Mark's web site at www.marklitwak.com, where you can find more about his books and read many helpful articles that he has written and posted for filmmakers like you.

Mark, in your article you talk about several ways to finance films. Which would you say is the most common and why?

There are several ways to finance films including by territory presales, investors, studio funds or some combination. Many documentaries are funded with grants and donations,

The popularity of each financing method varies over time. At one time, a lot of presales were being used to finance production but right now it is very hard to do presales because the German market is depressed, and Germany has historically been a country that pays a large license fee.

Now filmmakers are relying on equity money for financing and production incentives such as tax breaks and refunds from various countries that help subsidize the making of a film.

Is Canada still subsidizing productions?

Yes, Canada provides incentives and so do many other countries. In addition to the incentives offered, there is also a favorable exchange rate when converting U.S. dollars to Canadian dollars, which is an added attraction. Likewise, in some countries in Eastern Europe production expenses are so low that the net effect is similar to shooting in a country offering a generous incentive.

Have you heard that the New Zealand Film Commission will match up to $2.5 million in funds if your film has "strong New Zealand" content and uses New Zealand people on the crew and for post?

I know that both New Zealand and Australia have very popular programs to encourage production. We have an extensive listing of production incentives available in various countries including New Zealand and Australia, and also have a listing of the incentives various states offer. Both are posted on my website: Entertainment Legal Resources at www.marklitwak.com.

Mark, how early in the production do you believe filmmakers should see an attorney?

It depends on the experience of the filmmaker. For a first time filmmaker, pretty early. If it is an experienced filmmaker, he or she may not need help for a while. There are some filmmakers who may have a legal education and lots of practical experience who may never need help from an attorney.

I know of cases where filmmakers did not get the appropriate releases and paperwork and ended up spending more on attorneys later in the production than they would have if they had consulted with one early in production.

That's often the case. Sometimes filmmakers produce a film and cannot obtain distribution for it because they did not properly secure their copyright. I know of a producer who did not get a release from an actor, and then lost touch with that actor, and could not locate him. This caused problems when it came time to demonstrate to the distributor that the filmmaker had rights to the actor's work.

In some instances if you are raising money from third parties, you need to see an attorney before you accept funds to make sure you are complying with the law. If the person giving you the money is doing so because they are making an investment, their interest, is considered a security, unless the investor is actively involved in producing the film. And if securities are involved, then you need to comply with state and federal securities laws. You may need to make certain disclosures, which is usually done via a private placement memorandum (PPM). This document discloses all the risks of the investment to potential investors before you accept their money.

If someone wants to give you money as a gift, that is, with no expectations or obligations attached, *mazel tov*! Take the gift and thank them - you don't have to comply with the laws that govern investments, although gifts are sometimes taxable, and the gift giver may want to obtain a tax deduction.

In documentaries there are often donations of money for in-kind services. There may be gifts from family or friends or charitable contributions. In order for the person making the gift to receive a tax deduction they may want to give the money to a 501(c)3 corporation, a type of non-profit entity. If you don't have your own 501(c)3 corporation, you can arrange with an existing one to serve as an umbrella organization for you. The International Documentary Association offers this service. They will accept the money, take a small administrative fee, and then pass the funds on to the filmmaker. This enables the gift giver to receive a tax deduction and allows the filmmaker to make their film.

How should you handle gifts?

If someone is making a gift, that should be clear to both parties up front. It is a good idea to have the donor confirm in writing that a gift is intended. If they are giving you money and they expect to share in any kind of revenues from the film, then it is not a gift, but an investment. If the film does not generate revenue, then the investment may be a write-off, and the investor may be able to take it as a loss on their income tax return. Remember, films are risky investments.

When someone is making a gift there are usually few legal issues involved, for example a large gift might be subject to gift tax. But investments are governed by complex security laws at the state and federal level that try to protect investors from being defrauded and taken advantage of.

When filmmakers bring their film ideas to you, do you help them with the investment package?

Yes, we prepare the private placement memorandum and related documents.

Does the filmmaker give you the creative side?

Yes, in preparing the PPM the client supplies the synopsis of the story, a budget summary, and bios of the people involved. We take care of all of the legal disclosures, and all of the descriptions of how the movie business works, all the risk factors, and all the required legal notices.

What about ancillary rights of books or music? Does this go into the original package?

If you are making a feature, then ancillary rights and other sources of revenue can include home video, TV, book novelizations, soundtrack albums, merchandising etc. The filmmaker can include these sources of revenue in the film's gross receipts and share them with investors. They can also be excluded from the revenues shared with investors, but this may discourage investors from participation in the project. At any rate, revenue from ancillary sources needs to be addressed when dealing with investors.

Have you been successful in helping filmmakers find funding once you have created the package?

We are lawyers, not investment bankers or fundraisers. The task of raising financing is usually borne by the producer. The attorney makes sure the producer is complying with the law.

What is gap financing? Is it still popular?

Gap financing has to do with financing based on presales. Presales are when a filmmaker or a distributor approaches a distributor for a country, before the film is produced, and persuades this distributor to sign a contract to pay a license fee for the distribution rights to the film when it is completed. If the contracts are with reputable and solvent distributors, the filmmaker can use these contracts as collateral for a production loan. The filmmaker borrows money from a bank, which may lend eighty to ninety percent of the licensee fees in the contracts.

The filmmaker produces the film and delivers it to the distributors who have licensed it. The distributors pay their license fee to the bank that lent the funds to the producer. The filmmaker can make additional sales and earn profits from licenses to unsold territories.

Gap financing is when the bank is lending you more money than the value of the presale contracts. Let's say you make distribution deals for Germany, Spain and Italy. The total face value of all these distribution deals is $500,000. But you need to borrow $600,000 to produce your film. The difference between the amount covered by licensee fees in the contracts, and the amount borrowed, is the gap. Banks charge additional interest for covering this gap because they are taking greater risk. If the film is made and you don't enter into any other licensing agreements, then the bank may suffer a loss. Gap financing is therefore more expensive to the filmmaker.

I noticed that most producers create a Limited Liability Company instead of a C or S Corporation. Why is this?

An LLC is a relatively new vehicle, and has some advantages over a corporate form of organization in that it allows the profits and losses to be passed through to the members without being taxed at the company level. This avoids the problem of double taxation that you might have with a C corporation where the income for the corporation is taxed, and then the same money is taxed again when paid out in the form of dividends to investors. This reduces the flow of

110

money back to the investors Another way to avoid double taxation is to set up a partnership, which passes profits and losses through to the partners. Here there is no taxation at the company level. But the problem with partnerships is that there is no limited liability for the general partners, only for the limited partners. So the general partners may be concerned that they may lose their houses or other assets if they are sued because the company has defaulted on its contractual obligations.

By setting up an LLC you have all of the advantages of the partnership form of business without the liability exposure imposed on the general partners. In an LLC you have managing members of the LLC, who are typically the producers, and the non-managing members, who are the investors. They both receive limited liability and there's no double taxation because the LLC can elect to have the IRS treat it like a partnership for tax purposes, that is, all the profits and losses pass through to the members. That's why the LLC form of business has become so popular. But LLCs are not always appropriate. In some instances it may be wiser to set up a corporation or a partnership, or use some other business entity.

Do you see theatres moving to digital cinema in the future?

I think that there will be more and more theatres that can exhibit pictures digitally. Ultimately, movies will also be distributed digitally, which will result in much more efficient and cost effective means of distribution than the present system of shipping prints. Digital distribution could be accomplished by beaming the picture by satellite from the studio directly to the theatres where it will be captured on a computer hard disk and then exhibited. Information such as how many times the movie was shown could be beamed back to the distributor. The studios will be able to

111

avoid the expense of having to ship thousands of 35mm celluloid prints to theaters and back, and they won't have to pay for environmentally sound disposal of old prints. The major studios could probably save close to a billion dollars a year in print and distribution expenses if films were digitally distributed.

One could also distribute ditigally over an Internet or broadband connection, or by shipping packaged media, such as a DVD, to a theater. That would be less expensive than shipping a 35mm print, which is quite heavy and bulky.

The big obstacle to digital cinema is that most of the savings of changing to a digital distribution system inures to the benefit of the distributors - the studios - but the cost for buying digital projection equipment and servers, which are fairly expensive, is an expense that has traditionally been borne by theatre owners - the exhibitors.

Exhibitors already have 35mm projectors, which last many years, and they are not anxious to spend more money to install digital technology in their theatres if most of the savings go to the studios. So until the exhibitors have a financial incentive to go digital, the transformation is going to be slow. The distributors will have to come up with a way to share the money saved with exhibitors. Theatre owners don't want to spend all of this money just so the studios can make more money.

The theatre owners don't see a return on their investment from new digital equipment?

If someone comes to your theatre and sees the movie on a digital screen instead of from a traditional screen, they pay the same price for a ticket and some popcorn. So from the point of view of the local theatre owner, why pay $50,000 to install a digital projection system if it doesn't generate any additional revenue?

Would you say we are going to experience an explosion of low-budget films on the market due to the new digital technology?

It has happened already. There are an enormous number of low budget films being made on digital media. Some of the digital media is better than others. The 24 P-high definition cameras have very good quality. The lower level stuff is not quite as good, but people are able to make their movies for much less money than shooting on film. By shooting digitally, you don't have to pay for developing and processing. Plus the digital cameras are inexpensive.

What legal advice would you give to a first time filmmaker?

I think it really depends on the filmmaker and their level of industry expertise. Filmmakers need to spend a lot of time perfecting their craft as a filmmaker, and also gain an understanding of the business side of the industry, including what they can and cannot do legally. They need to know what sort of rights they need to secure in order to make a film, and how to protect themselves from liability. They can do this by consulting an attorney or by reading and educating themselves.

I have written a book called *Dealmaking in the Film and Television Industry*, which is a primer for filmmakers to learn about many of the legal issues involved in production.

Is this available on your web site at www.marklitwak.com?

Yes, and at Amazon.com and most bookstores. It is widely available. The publisher is Silman-James Press.

Would you call this book Filmmaking Legalities 101?

Yes, it definitely is.

Carole Joyce

Living in heaven

FINANCING INDEPENDENT FILMS
by Mark Litwak

The following was written and edited by Mark Litwak.

Independent films can be financed in a variety of ways. In addition to filmmakers using their own funds to make a movie, the most common methods are: 1) loans; 2) investor financing; 3) borrowing against pre-sales (a loan against distribution contracts); and 4) distributor-supplied financing.

LOANS

Loans can be secured or unsecured. A secured loan is supported or backed by security or collateral. When one takes out a car or home loan, the loan is secured by that property. If the person who borrows money fails to repay the loan, the creditor may take legal action to have the collateral sold and the proceeds applied to pay off the debt.

An unsecured loan has no particular property backing it. Credit card debt and loans from family or friends may be unsecured. If a debtor defaults on an unsecured loan, the creditor can sue for repayment and force the sale of the debtor's assets to repay the loan. If the debtor has many

---

[1] THESE MATERIALS ARE OFFERED FOR USE AS A TEACHING TOOL ONLY. THEY ARE DESIGNED TO HELP YOU UNDERSTAND SOME OF THE LEGAL ISSUES YOU MAY ENCOUNTER IN THE ENTERTAINMENT BUSINESS AND ENABLE YOU TO BETTER COMMUNICATE WITH YOUR LAWYER. THEY ARE NOT OFFERED AS LEGAL ADVICE, NOR SHOULD THEY BE CONSTRUED AS SUCH. THEY ARE NOT A SUBSTITUTE FOR CONSULTING WITH AN ATTORNEY AND RECEIVING ADVICE BASED ON YOUR FACTS AND CIRCUMSTANCES. MOREOVER, THE CASES AND LAWS CITED ARE SUBJECT TO CHANGE AND THEY MAY NOT APPLY IN ALL JURISDICTIONS.

debts, however, the sale of his property may not be sufficient to satisfy all creditors. In such a case, creditors may end up receiving only a small portion of the money owed them.

A secured creditor is in a stronger position to receive repayment. In the event of a default, designated property (the secured property) will be sold and all the proceeds will be applied first to repay the secured creditor's debt. Unsecured creditors will share in whatever is left, if anything.

The advantage of a loan, from a legal point of view, is that the transaction can often be structured in a fairly simple and inexpensive manner. A short promissory note can be used and the transaction often is not subject to the complex security laws that govern many investments. Thus, there is usually no need to prepare a private placement memorandum (PPM). Keep in mind that if the agreement between the parties is labeled a "loan," but in reality it is an investment, the courts will likely view the transaction as an investment. Giving a creditor a "piece of the back-end," or otherwise giving the creditor equity in the project, makes the transaction look like an investment.

The difference between a loan and an investment has to do with risk. With a loan, the entity that borrows funds, the debtor, is obligated to repay the loan and whatever interest is charged, regardless of whether the film is a flop or a hit. The creditor earns interest but does not share in the upside potential (*i.e.*, profits) of a hit. Since the creditor is entitled to repayment even if the film is a flop, the creditor does not share in the risk of the endeavor. Of course, there is some risk with a loan because loans are not always repaid, especially unsecured loans that don't have any collateral backing them. That risk is minimal, however, compared to the risk of an equity investment.

In a pre-sale agreement, a buyer licenses or pre-buys movie distribution rights for a territory before the film has been produced. The deal works something like this: Filmmaker Henry approaches Distributor Juan to sign a contract to buy the right to distribute Henry's next film. Henry gives Juan a copy of the script and tells him the names of the principal cast members.

Juan has distributed several of Henry's films in the past. He paid $50,000 for the right to distribute Henry's last film in Spain. The film did reasonably well and Juan feels confident, based on Henry's track record, the script, and the proposed cast, that his next film should also do well in Spain. Juan is willing to license Henry's next film sight unseen before it has been produced. By buying distribution rights to the film now, Juan is obtaining an advantage over competitors who might bid for it. Moreover, Juan may be able to negotiate a lower license fee than what he would pay if the film were sold on the open market. So Juan signs a contract agreeing to buy Spanish distribution rights to the film. Juan does not have to pay (except if a deposit is required) until completion and delivery of the film to him.

Henry now takes this contract, and a dozen similar contracts with buyers to the bank. Henry asks the bank to lend him money to make the movie with the distribution contracts as collateral. Henry is "banking the paper." The bank will not lend Henry the full face value of the contracts, but instead will discount the paper and lend a smaller sum. So if the contracts provide for a cumulative total of $1,000,000 in license fees, the bank might lend Henry $800,000. In some circumstances banks are willing lend more than the face value of the contracts (so-called gap financing) and charge higher fees.

Henry uses this money to produce his film. When the movie is completed, he delivers it to the companies that have already licensed it. They in turn pay their license fees to Henry's bank to retire Henry's loan. The bank receives repayment of its loan plus interest. The buyers receive the right to distribute the film in their territory. Henry can now license the film in territories that remain unsold. From these revenues Henry makes his profit.

Juan's commitment to purchase the film must be un-equivocal, and his company financially secure, so that a bank is willing to lend Henry money on the strength of Juan's promise and ability to pay. If the contract merely states that the buyer will review and consider purchasing the film, this commitment is not strong enough to borrow against. Banks want to be assured that the buyer will accept delivery of the film as long as it meets certain technical standards, even if artistically the film is a disappointment. The bank will also want to know that Juan's company is fiscally solid and likely to be in business when it comes time for it to pay the license fee. If Juan's company has been in business for many years, and if the company has substantial assets on its balance sheet, the bank will usually lend against the contract.

The bank often insists on a completion bond to ensure that the filmmaker has sufficient funds to finish the film. Banks are not willing to take much risk. They know that Juan's commitment to buy Henry's film is contingent on delivery of a completed film. But what if Henry goes over budget and cannot finish the film? If Henry doesn't deliver the film, Juan is not obligated to pay for it, and the bank is not repaid its loan.

To avoid this risk, the bank wants an insurance company, the completion guarantor, to agree to put up any money needed to complete the film should it go over budget. Before issuing a policy, a completion guarantor will carefully review the proposed budget and the track record of key production personnel. Unless the completion guarantor is confident that the film can be brought in on budget, no policy will issue. These policies are called completion bonds.

First-time filmmakers may find it difficult to finance their films through pre-sales. With no track record of successful films to their credit, they may not be able to persuade a distributor to pre-buy their work. How does the distributor know that the filmmaker can produce something their audiences will want to see? Of course, if the other elements are strong, the distributor may be persuaded to take that risk. For example, even though the filmmaker may be a first-timer, if the script is from an acclaimed writer, and several big name actors will participate, the overall package may be attractive.

The terms of an agreement between the territory buyer (licensor) and the international distributor can be quite complex. A sample license agreement is presented at the end of this chapter.

Parties may disagree about the meaning of terms used in their agreements. The following terms are standard AFMA definitions, which are generally accepted in the industry. They are used to interpret whatever document they are attached to.

EQUITY INVESTMENTS

An equity investment can be structured in a number of ways. For example, an investor could be a stockholder in a corporation, a non-managing member of a Limited Liability Company (LLC), or a limited partner in a partnership.

An investor shares in potential rewards as well as the risks of failure. If a movie is a hit, the investor is entitled to receive his investment back and share in proceeds as well. Of course, if the movie is a flop, the investor may lose his entire investment. The producer is not obligated to repay an investor his loss.

The interests of individuals and companies that do not manage the enterprise they invest in are known as securities. These investors may be described using a variety of terms including silent partners, limited partners, passive investors and stockholders. They are putting money into a business that they are not managing (*i.e.*, not running). State

119

and federal securities laws are designed to protect such investors by ensuring that the people managing the business (*e.g.*, the general partners in a partnership or the officers and directors of a corporation) do not defraud investors by giving them false or misleading information, or by failing to disclose information that a reasonably prudent investor would want to know.

In a limited partnership agreement, for example, investors (limited partners) put up the money needed to produce a film. Investors usually desire limited liability. That is, they don't want to be financially responsible for any cost overruns or liability that might arise if, for instance, a stunt person is injured. They want their potential loss limited to their investment.

Because limited partnership interests are considered securities, they are subject to state and federal securities laws. These laws are complex and have strict requirements. A single technical violation can subject general partners to liability. Therefore, it is important that filmmakers retain an attorney with experience in securities work and familiarity with the entertainment industry. This is one area where filmmakers should not attempt to do it themselves.

Registration and Exemptions

The federal agency charged with protecting investors is the U.S. Securities and Exchange Commission (SEC). Various state and federal laws require that most securities be registered with state and/or federal governments. Registration for a public offering is time-consuming and expensive, and not a realistic alternative for most low-budget filmmakers. Filmmakers can avoid the expense of registration if they qualify for one or more statutory exemptions. These exemptions are generally restricted to private placements, which entail approaching people one already knows (*i.e.*, the parties have a pre-existing relationship). Compare a private placement with a public offering where offers can be made to strangers, such as soliciting the public at large through advertising. Generally, a public offering can only be made after the U.S. Securities and Exchange Commission (SEC) has reviewed and approved it.

There are a variety of exemptions to federal registration. For example, there is an exemption for intrastate offerings limited to investors all of whom reside within one state. To qualify for the intrastate offering exemption, a company must: be incorporated in the state where it is offering the securities, and it must carry out a significant amount of its business in that state. There is no fixed limit on the size of the offering or the number of purchasers. Relying solely on this exemption can be risky, however, because if an offer is made to a single non-resident the exemption could be lost.

Under SEC Regulation D (Reg D) there are three exemptions from federal registration. These can permit filmmakers to offer and sell their securities without having to register the securities with the SEC. These exemptions are under Rules 504, 505 and 506 of Regulation D. While companies relying on a Reg D exemption do not have to register their securities and usually do not have to file reports with the SEC, they must file a document known as Form D when they first sell their securities. This document gives notice of the names and addresses of the company's owners and promoters. State laws also apply and the offeror will likely need to file a document with the appropriate state agency for every state in which an investor resides.

Investors considering an investment in an offering under Reg D can contact the SEC's Public Reference Branch at (202) 942-8090 or send an email to publicinfo@sec.gov to determine whether a company has filed Form D, and to obtain a copy. A potential investor may also want to check with his/her state regulator to see if the offering has complied with state regulations. State regulators can be contacted through the North American Securities Administrators Association at (202) 737-0900 or by visiting its website

at http://www.nasaa.org/nasaa/abtnasaa/
find_regulator.html.

Information about the SEC's registration requirements and exemptions is available at

http://www.sec.gov/info/smallbus/qasbsec.htm.

An "offering" is usually comprised of several documents including a private placement memorandum (PPM), a proposed limited partnership agreement (or operating agreement for an LLC, or bylaws for a corporation), and an investor questionnaire used to determine if the investor is qualified to invest. A PPM contains the type of information usually found in a business plan, and a whole lot more. It is used to disclose the essential facts that a reasonable investor would want to know before making an investment. The offeror may be liable if there are any misrepresentations in the PPM, or any omissions of material facts.

State registration can be avoided by complying with the requirements for limited offering exemptions under state law. These laws are often referred to as "Blue Sky" laws. They were enacted after the stock market crash that occurred during the Great Depression. They are designed to protect investors from being duped into buying securities that are worthless - backed by nothing more than the blue sky.

The above-mentioned federal and state exemptions may restrict offerors in several ways. Sales are typically limited to 35 non-accredited investors, and the investors may need to have a pre-existing relationship with the issuer (or investment sophistication adequate to understand the transaction), the purchasers cannot purchase for resale, and advertising or general solicitation is generally not permitted. There is usually no numerical limit on the number of accredited investors.

A "pre-existing relationship" is defined as any relationship consisting of personal or business contacts of a nature and duration such as would enable a reasonably prudent purchaser to be aware of the character, business acumen and general business and financial circumstances of the person with whom the relationship exists.

Other documents may need to be filed with federal and state governments. For example, a Certificate of Limited Partnership may need to be filed with the Secretary of State to establish a partnership. In California, a notice of the transaction and consent to service of process is filed with the Department of Corporations. If the transaction is subject to federal law, Form D will need to be filed with the Securities and Exchange Commission (SEC) soon after the first and last sales. Similar forms may need to be filed in every state in which any investor resides.

In the independent film business, PPMs are usually: a Rule 504 offering to raise up to $1,000,000, or a Rule 505 offering which allows the filmmaker to raise up to $5,000,000, or a Rule 506 offering which doesn't have a monetary cap on the amount of funds to be raised. A 506 offering also offers the advantage of preempting state laws under the provisions of the National Securities Markets Improvement Act of 1996 ("NSMIA").

504 Offering

Under Rule 504, offerings may be exempt from registration for companies when they offer and sell up to $1,000,000 of their securities in a 12-month period.

A company can use this exemption so long as it is not a so-called blank check company, which is one that has no specific business plan or purpose. The exemption generally does not allow companies to solicit or advertise to the public, and purchasers receive restricted securities, which they cannot sell to others without registration or an applicable exemption.

Under certain limited circumstances, Rule 504 does permit companies to make a public offering of tradable securities. For example, if a company registers the offering exclusively in states that require a publicly filed registration statement and delivery of a substantive disclosure document to investors; or if the company sells exclusively according to state law exemptions that permit general solicitation, provided the company sells only to accredited investors.

505 Offering

Under a Rule 505 exemption, a company can offer and sell up to $5,000,000 of its securities in any 12-month period. It may sell to an unlimited number of "accredited investors" and up to 35 non-accredited investors who do not need to satisfy the sophistication or wealth standards associated with other exemptions. The company must inform investors that they are receiving restricted securities that cannot be sold for at least a year without registering them. General solicitation and advertising is prohibited.

Rule 505 allows companies to decide what information to give to accredited investors, so long as it does not violate the antifraud prohibitions of federal securities laws. But companies must give non-accredited investors disclosure documents that are comparable to those used in registered offerings. If a company provides information to accredited investors, it must provide the same information to non-accredited investors. The offeror must also be available to answer questions from prospective investors.

506 Offering

Under Rule 506, one can raise an unlimited amount of capital. However, the offeror cannot engage in any public solicitation or advertising. There is no limit as to the number of accredited investors that can participate. However, only 35 non-accredited investors can participate.

Accredited investors include (among others) the following:

a. any natural persons whose individual net worth, or joint net worth with that person's spouse, at the time of the purchase exceeds $1,000,000;

b. any natural person with an individual income in the two prior years and an estimated income in the current year in excess of $200,000 or joint income with spouse of $300,000;

c. any director, executive officer, or general partner of the issuer of the securities being offered or sold, or any director, executive officer or partner of a general partner of the issuer;

Under Rule 506, each purchaser of units must be "sophisticated," as that term is defined under federal law. Note that an "accredited investor" is not the same as "sophisticated" investor. The term "accredited investor" is specifically defined by the federal securities laws, while the term "sophisticated investor" has no precise legal definition. Both terms generally refer to an investor who has a sufficiently high degree of financial knowledge and expertise such that he/she does not need the protections afforded by the SEC. An investor who is considered "sophisticated," might not meet the precise definition of an accredited investor.

As with Rule 505 offerings, it is up to the offeror to decide what information is given to accredited investors, provided there is no violation of the anti-fraud provisions. Non-accredited investors must be given disclosure documents similar to those used in registered offerings. If the offeror provides information to accredited investors, the same information must be given to non-accredited investors. The offeror must be available to answer questions by prospective purchasers.

Under Rule 506, each purchaser must represent that he or she is purchasing the units for his or her own investment only and not with plans to sell or otherwise distribute the units. The units purchased are "restricted" and may not be resold by the investor except in certain circumstances.

Intrastate Offering Exemption

Section 3(a)(11) of the Securities Act provides for an intrastate offering exemption. This exemption is designed for the financing of local businesses. To qualify for the intrastate offering exemption, a company needs to be incorporated in the state where it is offering the securities; carry out a significant amount of its business in that state; and make offers and sales only to residents of that state.

There is no fixed limit on the size of the offering or the number of purchasers. The company needs to carefully determine the residence of each purchaser. If any of the securities are offered or sold to even one out-of-state person, the exemption may be lost. Moreover, if an investor resells any of the securities to a person who resides out of state within a short period of time after the company's offering is complete (the usual test is nine months), the entire transaction, including the original sales, might violate the Securities Act.

Accredited Investor Exemption

Section 4(6) of the Securities Act exempts from registration offers and sales of securities to accredited investors when the total offering price is less than $5,000,000.

The definition of accredited investors is the same as that used under Regulation D. Like the exemptions in Rule 505 and 506, this exemption does not permit any public solicitation. There are no document delivery requirements but the anti-fraud provisions mentioned below do apply.

California Limited Offering Exemption

SEC Rule 1001 exempts from registration offers and sales of securities, in amounts of up to $5,000,000, which satisfies the conditions of §25102(n) of the California Corporations Code. This California law exempts from California state law registration offerings made by California companies to "qualified purchasers" whose characteristics are similar to, but not the same as, accredited investors under Regulation D. This exemption allows some methods of general solicitation prior to sales.

ANTI-FRAUD PROVISIONS

All security offerings, even those exempt from registration under Reg. D, are subject to the antifraud provisions of the federal securities laws, and any applicable state antifraud provisions. Consequently, the offeror will be responsible for any false or misleading statements, whether oral or written. Those who violate the law can be pursued under both criminally and civilly. Moreover, an investor who has purchased a security on the basis of misleading information, or the omission of relevant information, can rescind the investment agreement and obtain a refund of his/her investment.

Mark Litwak is a veteran entertainment attorney with offices in Beverly Hills, California. He is the author of five books including: Reel Power, The Struggle for Influence and Success in the New Hollywood, Courtroom Crusaders, Dealmaking in the Film and Television Industry (winner of the 1995 Kraszna-Krausz Moving Image Book Award), Contracts for the Film and Television Industry, and Litwak's Multimedia Producer's Handbook.

Mr. Litwak has been interviewed on more than 100 television and radio shows including ABC, "The Larry King Show," National Public Radio's "All Things Considered," and CNN Network. He wrote, co-produced and directed the feature length award-winning documentary "Ralph Nader: Up Close," which was broadcast on PBS stations, and he has packaged various movie projects and served as executive producer on such recently completed feature films as "The Proposal," "Out of Line" and "Pressure."

ALTERNATIVE FINANCING: Projects With Non Traditional Partners

If you're going to survive as a producer, you need to arm yourself with knowledge. You need to keep up with the latest trends, and familiarize yourself with the entire gamut of marketing techniques and strategies that are available. Above all, you must use your creativity to invent new strategies. Forums and conferences are a great place to exchange creative ideas and explore what's working and what's not working.

RealScreen invited me to speak about our Roy W. Dean film and video grants at their 2002 New York conference. I had heard great things about the *RealScreen* conferences and wanted to attend one for quite some time, but just couldn't manage to squeeze it into my schedule. I'm glad I finally did because I was blown away by how much I learned in just two days. As a matter of fact, I found this conference to be such a valuable resource that I have decided to include it in my annual itinerary of places to fuel-up on the latest information, take in valuable networking time, and enjoy some wonderful food.

Patric Hedlund, author of *A Bread Crumb Trail Through the PBS Jungle: The Producer's Survival Guide*, gave a keynote address, and Peter Kaufman moderated a dynamic forum on Alternative Financing.

---

* Reviewed at http://www.forests.com/breadcrumb

Peter has been actively involved in the media industry for over eighteen years. He is a Senior Fellow for Media and International Affairs at the World Policy Institute of New School University in New York, and he is a member of the Editorial Board on the *World Policy Journal*.

Peter is also the founder and president of *Intelligent Television*, where he advises producers and networks on issues pertaining to the licensing and merchandising of ancillary products. According to Peter, producers can successfully raise money for their projects by acquiring funds from unlikely sponsors like record companies, book and magazine publishers, authors, and other corporations.

Several panel members shared success stories on how they were able to generate revenue by tapping into the intellectual property markets of the music or publishing industries through companies like *Reader's Digest, Sony,* and *Simon & Schuster*.

Keith Lawrence is a partner at *Timeline Films*, and the Chief Financial Officer and Secretary of the *Mary Pickford Foundation*. Keith was a salesman and a theatre director when Ferde Grofe came to one of his plays and asked if he would like to be a partner in a new film adventure, *Aviation AV Library*. This partnership allowed Keith to start making documentary films back in 1979, before cable networks like *Discovery* and the *History Channel* had created a marketing niche for documentaries.

When Keith and his partner decided to produce a film about flying, he went to the Army and Navy film archives, borrowed public domain footage of aviation films, streamed the footage together into a video, then set off to find a market for his newest documentary. Keith knew that most magazines had leftover ad space just before they went to press, so he went to *Aviation Week* and offered to give them 20% from the sale of his video in return for some advertising space.

The very first month he had 150 orders for tapes at $99 per hour. By end of year he had 16 magazines running ads, and was selling 10,000 videocassettes. That's an incredible profit! Especially when you consider that his only expense was the cost of editing and dubbing. Naturally people began to copy his marketing strategy, so Keith had to go outside the box once again to create another new marketing approach.

In 1981, while reading an article in *Reader's Digest*, Keith begin to think about how he might use the magazine's marketing strategy to his favor. The magazine offered readers various premiums as incentives, so Keith contacted the promotions department and asked if they would consider using his documentary as one of the premiums. They told him they did not have the resources to support the duplicating process but Keith refused to accept defeat.

He dug deeper and found out that the Department of Research and Development at *Reader's Digest* conducted various marketing surveys. This gave him an idea. Keith was confident that Americans would choose documentary programs for premiums if they were given the opportunity, so he told *Reader's Digest* that he would produce a thousand tapes at his own expense if they would test his idea in their next survey. The average marketing survey can take up to 12 months, but the public's response to Keith's documentary was so favorable that it took *Reader's Digest* just over three months to become the first publisher to offer a documentary film as a premium.

Keith didn't sit back and rest on his laurels. He went back to the to the Army and Navy film archives, acquired more footage, and went to work editing his newest documentary, *War in the Pacific*. Even Keith was surprised by the orders that begin to pour in. His first order was for 30,000 tapes! Soon Keith was knocking on the door of every magazine publisher he could find. At first they were hesitant to let him in, but Keith persisted and within a year his documentaries were listed in over 250 magazines.

The story doesn't end there. A marketing executive for *US News and World Report* purchased a copy of *War in the Pacific* for her father through the *Reader's Digest* premium program. She liked Keith's film so much that she tracked him down and asked him if he would be interested in participating in a similar promotional program with *US News and World Report*. Keith responded with a new documentary called *War Aces*. The executive was so impressed that she took the promotional video to *A&E* and sold them on the idea of running a series based on Keith's documentary.

The result was a 12-part series called *Air Combat*, a new beginning for *A&E*, who had previously only aired biographies, and a new beginning for Keith in the broadcast television market. Keith found success because he was open to new markets as well as new marketing strategies. He was constantly working to get his product out there where it would be seen. Keith's perseverance paid off when he captured the attention of someone who was passionate about his films.

Keith believes one of the keys to success is finding support from individuals who share a passion for your idea. According to Keith, the most important issue is not what the cable channels are doing, or what other filmmakers are doing. Keith says the most important thing is that the filmmaker has passion, and the ability to find support from people who share this passion. This philosophy certainly worked for him!

During the conference entertainment attorney, Robert Freedman, encouraged producers to embrace a new way of thinking. Mr. Freedman is the author of the leading formbook on television contracts, *Entertainment Industry Contracts: Television*, published by Matthew Bender, and is a contributing editor to *Entertainment Law and Finance* and *Broadcast Law Reports*. He represents award-winning filmmakers, television producers, and a broad array of industry talent, including writers, directors, performers and composers.

Freedman said documentary filmmakers must do away with the "tin cup" approach to fundraising, and they must stop thinking of themselves as the "poor cousins of feature filmmakers." According to Freedman, approaching potential donors with lines like, "this is a wonderful project, and we really need your money," might be an appropriate fundraising technique for the local church or synagogue, but it is not effective or appropriate for today's entertainment market. Freedman encourages documentary filmmakers to think of their project as a vehicle that potential funders can use to meet *their* goals and the key to successful prospecting is finding the right hook.

If you were doing a small documentary series on large cats around the world, your obvious market would be a channel like *Discovery*, *HBO*, or *Animal Planet*. Freedman says you might as well take a number because you are going to have to get in line with hundreds of other filmmakers who are there for the same reason.

Freedman challenges filmmakers to take a different tactic when approaching stations. Instead of asking for money, ask for airtime. Think of your project as a vehicle for some entity and turn to corporations and businesses to explore different methods of creative financing.

Look at all the manufacturers and companies who exploit majestic big cats through advertising campaigns and get ready to pounce. Stalk *MGM* or *Exxon*, after all, they've reduced the king of beasts to a mascot, turn-about is fair play! How about *Mercury Motors*, maker of the *Jaguar*? If your series is called *The World of Big Cats*, anything with the word "world" in it is fair game.

The key is you must be able to pitch these companies with a dynamic concept for a film in one hand, and an enticing incentive that will benefit their corporation in the other. It's not, "what can you do for my documentary?" It's "look what my documentary can do for you!"

Put together a charitable benefit for a cat that is on the endangered list. You will be promoting your film, your corporate sponsor, and helping an endangered animal with one activity.

Don't stop there! Write a heart-tugging story about the plight of your endangered cat and offer the exclusive rights to a national magazine. Ask the publisher to give you a full-page ad in the next issue in lieu of payment, then double-dip your creativity. Take your article, along with the publisher's agreement and a sample copy of the magazine, to potential donors and show them how their donation of $10,000 will give their corporation a credit on an important documentary about an endangered animal, *then show them how great their name and logo is going to look next to your film on that full page ad.* Find out how much they would pay for this type of advertising before you go and show them the figures. They can't lose!

Your web site is another great advertising tool. Win potential sponsors by showing them how you can promote their corporation through your website. Do your homework and demonstrate how you plan to target their customer base and bring them to your web site. Direct web advertising like this is very important to corporations.

Explore product placement. Who can forget that memorable scene in *E.T.* when Elliott lured the shy alien into the house using *Reese's Pieces* as bait? You can bet the marketing executive at *M&M's* who turned Steven Spielberg away will never forget!

Mr. Freedman encourages filmmakers to explore the different products they will use during production and approach these corporations for help. If you are traveling in a *Jeep*, contact *Jeep*. If you are flying to your location, contact an airline for travel benefits. If you are taking stills, contact *Nikon*. If you need hotel rooms, call *Hilton*. Approach each of these corporations with a well thought out strategy for funding and product placement.

Use your creativity. Think your project through from beginning to end. Think about every stage of production, and consider all lateral advertising concepts. If your film promotes anything that relates in name or concept to any major corporation target that corporation for funding.

Documentary filmmakers should also explore opportunities in the feature film market. Freedman has had two clients sell the feature film rights to their documentary projects. Two of my *Roy W. Dean Grant* winners also negotiated successful sales for the feature film rights to their projects. This is a marketing strategy that is becoming more and more common so think about this possibility for your film.

Freedman talked about opportunities in the ancillary markets. Don't overlook the potential for selling the literary rights to book publishers, or funding your film by marketing the soundtrack.

During the forum on alternative financing a panel member offered an interesting story and some advice on how to approach potential donors. He advised filmmakers to know the type of charities that wealthy people gravitate to, and told the story of a filmmaker who happened to know that Hugh Hefner was a fan of film restoration. The filmmaker went to Hefner and asked him to finance his film about silent film stars. Hefner was interested, so they went to UCLA and asked them to act as a nonprofit producer. Both Hefner and UCLA received kudos for their role in film restoration, the producers got their funding plus a salary, and they made the film they wanted. That would have been a great ending, but that was not the end of the story! The producers took their film to a music producer and negotiated a deal to sell the music from these old films.

As you can see, the path can lead in many directions. You must be willing to take the journey and explore every avenue. This is the kind of creativity you need to get your film made. Stories like this capture the concept behind *The Art of Funding Your Film.* Remember, the new millennium calls for a new way of thinking. You must be willing to step out of the box and embrace new concepts. You will find the funds you need and I guarantee your journey will be an enjoyable one.

Panelist Niki Vettel offered some excellent advice from her vast experience in marketing and distribution management, media management, and project development. Vettel, who is the founder and president of *RealityCheck Media Consulting*, was the Senior Vice President of Program Development at *American Program Service* (now *American Public Television*), where she created and produced some of public television's most successful specials and series before establishing her own successful consulting business in 1998.

Niki is currently involved in the development, production, and marketing of public television primetime pledge specials featuring best-selling authors like Dr. Wayne Dyer, Julie Morgenstern and Cheryl Richardson.

Niki told the audience that it is essential to take the correct approach when looking for someone to develop music for a film project. You must bring something to the table. What idea or concept do you have in mind, and what value will it bring to their core business?

According to Niki, the first thing a publisher or music professional will want to know is what your plans are for distribution. They want to know how many people are going to see your program, and they will want to know the concept behind your film.

The ratings for pledge specials are often lower than regular programming but audience members who watch programs that feature authors or performers tend to be book and record-buyers, so ratings don't necessarily correlate with the success of a pledge show. Publishers and recording companies know that PBS pledge drives sell their products.

Think about how pledge drives have affected the careers of some of the top performing artists. Yanni became huge after his video *Live at the Acropolis* aired repeatedly over public television stations nationwide during a PBS pledge drive. *The Three Tenors* PBS special from Rome remains a favorite to this day. Who could forget the September 1992 Moody Blues concert, *The Moody Blues: Live at Red Rocks*, when a full 88-piece symphony orchestra accompanied the legendary band during a live concert for the very first time? That concert became one of PBS's top pledge drives and the program was made into a PBS television special, home video release, and a live album. Audience response was so overwhelming that the band went on tour playing with symphony orchestras in every city in the U.S. The PBS fund drive established the Moody Blues as one of the top touring acts of the decade.

If you're interested in how you can get in on some of the action, Niki Vettel says the first thing you must do is familiarize yourself with the ins and outs of distribution and marketing. Producers must know what publishers and music executives are looking for. These industries are constantly searching for a way to exploit their client's name, but Niki cautions producers to be selective when searching for an artist or an author. Producers must work hard to match the right talent to the right vehicle to promote that talent. She also advised producers to set their sites on an artist or author who has already enjoyed some measure of success-preferably someone who has a new book or a new album to promote. It takes a great deal of time to nurture a professional. Just because an author wrote a best selling book does not guarantee that author will be well received as an expert in a documentary without the professional guidance of a good producer.

If Niki Vettel were sitting across from you right now she would tell you that the most important thing you need to know is what you don't know. When Niki came up with the concept for *Sessions at West 54th*, she knew she had a good idea. What she didn't know was how to make it all happen, so she went out and found professionals who had the expertise she lacked and she brought them onboard. She put together a great team that met the needs of the artists, the public television stations, and the viewers.

When looking for money, remember to explore sponsorships. Artists and authors want exposure more than anything else and money is no object if you can give them what they want. Give them exposure and they will follow you anywhere, but you must know the market and you must have a solid plan before you knock on their door.

When she needed to raise funds for a PBS pledge program starring Dr. Wayne Dyer she went back to the head of the home video company that funded the Andrew Weil pledge specials and landed the first $50,000 for her budget. The *Wisdom Channel* was a major supporter of Dr. Dyer's philosophy so she pitched them and walked away with another sponsor. An audiocassette company signed on because they wanted to produce the audiotapes. Niki also approached a pay-per-view station that was looking for a program that would attract a larger female audience, and landed even more support. Niki Vettel is a walking testimony to the concept, *filmmaking is a business of relationships.*

It takes perseverance and determination. Thomas Edison supposedly went through more than 10,000 different formulas while trying to invent the light bulb. When one of his financial backers asked him why he didn't just admit the idea was a failure and quit, Edison's said, "I have not failed. I've just found 10,000 ways that don't work." Every failure moved him closer to his goal. Niki Vettel wants filmmakers to keep this in mind as they move through the funding jungle.

PRODUCT PLACEMENT AND BRANDING

When someone mentions E.T. what immediately comes to mind?

A boy, a bicycle, and a loveable creature silhouetted against a magnificent full moon.

Think of your favorite film and chances are the image that pops into your head comes straight from the film's one-sheet-that coveted poster that once graced the walls of your favorite movie theater.

The silhouette of a lone fireman emerges from a background of searing flames.

"Silently behind a door, it waits.
One breath of oxygen and it explodes in a deadly rage.
In that instant it can create a hero...or cover a secret."

-BACKDRAFT-

The hands of a child and adult loosely entwined against a charcoal background which bears a faint typewritten list of names and numbers. The scene is cast in subtle shades of gray with the exception of the child's red sleeve.

-SHINDLER'S LIST-

From the hundreds of application I get a year, the ones that stay with me are the ones that include a picture, or one-sheet, representing the film's concept. Instant association; this is what you want from the very first day you start to work on your film. You will spend the next two or three years working to develop your ideas into tangible images that will project your message. Brand these images. Put your message into one identifiable picture that will promote your vision and then go out there and capture your audience. Use some of your seed money to commission an artist and create your very own one-sheet. *Sensory Lab* out of Toronto does this for the winners of my Roy W. Dean grants. Contact Carlos Kam at carloskam@telus.net and see what he can do for you.

I have my very own one-sheet, but I must go back a few years to tell you how I got it. I was blessed to have my great-grandmother with me for the first thirteen years of my life. Everyday I would race home from school and beg my Gigi to tell me stories about my great-great grandfather, Christopher Edward "Tobe" Odem. After Tobe's mother died his father quickly remarried, but according to Gigi, Tobe and his father's new bride didn't exactly get along. One afternoon after watching a band of cowboys ride through town, Tobe decided it was time to spread his wings. He rode out to join them and never looked back. He was 12 years old.

Tobe Odem was an American cowboy. One of those indomitable Texas spirits who rounded up longhorn by the hundreds, branded their hides then drove them across Indian territory forging the Chisholm Trail. As I sat and listened to Gigi's stories I would stare out the window and try to imagine what it was like to cross hundreds of miles of open prairie for months on end without running into one barbed wire fence. It must have been heaven!

I was always full of questions: "How did they find water? How did they find the trail? How did they know which way to go? Gigi smiled and told me that "Old Tom" showed them the way. Old Tom was not your ordinary steer. Once a fellow cattleman offered to buy Old Tom for $3000-a virtual fortune back in the 1800's. But Tobe wouldn't think of parting with his prized possession. Why Tobe was so proud of that crazy old steer that he decorated his horns with gold rings!

I listened wide-eyed as Gigi told me about the various outlaws who rode into Tobe Odem Ranch for some conversation and a bite to eat. According to the law of the old west when you had lunch outside visitors were always welcome. Outlaw or lawman, it made no difference. Amnesty always prevailed at lunch once you hung your gun belt on the fence post. No one judged around the big Odem table as hired hands, bandits, and the Odem family partook of the grub and lively conversation. As soon as lunch was over the outlaws would mount their horses and set off, most likely in the direction of the next train or closest bank.

Gigi's wonderful stories stayed with me long after I left Texas for the bright lights of Hollywood, but as the years flew by I found myself longing for a piece of my past. I decided an oil painting of Tobe Odem would serve to capture the spirit of my roots so I commissioned one of my favorite artists to do the job. Tobe couldn't oblige me by sitting for the portrait but I was confident the artist could capture his spirit if I introduced Tobe through the stories I had heard as a young child. I wrote them all down then searched through the archives of Dallas newspapers and through volumes of dusty old books to find more. When I had the vision I was looking for I gathered everything together and sent it off to the artist.

I know this is a long story to drive home the importance of a one-sheet but what can I tell you? I'm a Texan and telling tall tales runs in my blood! I could have sent the artist an old photo, but the point is, it takes more if you are going to project the right image. Through my research I learned things I never heard from my dear Gigi. I learned that Tobe lived with a mysterious American Indian woman, that he was a great friend to Chief Quanta Parker, and that his favorite horse was a beautiful Appaloosa. Tobe Odem 1858-1913. What an amazing life. And now it's all there in a magnificent portrait of Tobe sitting astride that beautiful horse.

Take the time to produce a one-sheet that represents the spirit of your film. Have postcards made and use them for *everything*. Put them on top of your proposals, use them for note cards, use them for greeting cards and calling cards, leave them on desks, counters, pass them around at film festivals. Be creative.

People retain information differently. People who are visual tend to store information in pictures, while people who are auditory seem to retain information better through listening. Then there are those who are tactile or kinesthetic. These people seem to absorb information easier through moving, doing and touching. Strive to reach people on each of these levels. I printed my one-sheet on heavy textured paper so family and friends could feel the old west as well as see it. *CRC Printers* (colorprep@crcprinting.com) in California does an excellent job. Be sure to tell them you are a filmmaker and that their services came highly recommended by Carole Dean at *From the Heart Productions*.

You need to get your film out there before you even start shooting. I once heard about a producer who went through her entire budget before she even stepped foot in the editing suite. She managed to scrape together $500 and guess what she did with it? She hired a publicist to do a write up in the New York Times, then she took that article and sent it to everyone she knew-friends, donors, associates-to let them know that her project was alive and well. This producer generated so much interest with that one article that she was able to raise the balance she needed to get her film completed.

Publicists are not just for the rich and famous. Use a publicist to do write-ups in the trades. Do this early in production and use these articles in your proposals and your portfolio. Publicity gets results. My favorite publicist is Tory Berger, friends@netzero. Tory is a spiritual man with impeccably high ethics. He is a pro and a treasure to work with. Never underestimate the power of publicity. Include advertising and promotion in your film's budget and start your campaign from day one, even if production is slated to last five years. The time to start advertising is yesterday.

Christopher (Tobe) Odem with Old Tom
by Bruce Marshall

It is no use saying 'we are doing our best.' You have got to succeed in doing what is necessary.

—Winston Churchill

A CONVERSATION WITH
Entertainment Professional,
Patricia Ganguzza

Patricia Ganguzza started out in the TV Spot Sales de-partment of NBC-TV in New York and later moved to the network's Los Angeles affiliate. Today Patricia is the President of AIM Productions, a full-service entertainment market-ing company where she oversees the business and develop-ment of product placement for over fifty corporate clients in-cluding Snapple Beverage Group, *The* Unilever Corporation, M&M Mars, Kraft Foods, Gateway, *and* Yahoo! *Patricia's na-tional promotions include* Paramount Pictures Rugrats, Warner Bros. Free Willy 1 and 2, Batman Returns and Batman Forever, Spielberg's Tiny Toons Adventures, MCA/ Universal Home Video's Jurassic Park, New Line Cinema's Teenage Mutant Ninja Turtles, Frequency, *and* Turner Home Entertainment's Christmas in Connecticut.

Patricia's schedule would make the most driven adult beg for mercy yet she took time out to sit down and talk to me about product placement and branding because she cares about filmmakers like you and she wants you to succeed. So sit back and learn from one of the most knowledgeable, well-respected people in the industry:

What do you say to young filmmakers who are per-haps a bit idealistic about the marriage between corpo-rations and the film industry?

I have spoken and taught classes at NYU Tisch specifi-cally about the business of filmmaking. It certainly is a business. I meet a lot of young filmmakers who think the only business part of filmmaking is the financing. I edu-cate them about the role corporations play in the production and marketing of the majority of films today. Hollywood and Corporate America shook hands a long time ago. Although filmmakers come with all of these ideals about not compromising the creativity of their film by having any influence by corporate sponsors, I always tell them it is nice to hold the ideal vision and not have to sacrifice your creativity but if you remain too rigid in that vein of thinking, your films may never get made. There is a creative way to involve corporations and their products without sacrificing your creative endeavor or compromising the creative vision.

There was a young French girl in one of my classes who said "I would never compromise by putting some brand name product in my film," and I said, "Well enjoy your film career whatever that is." I am telling you that this is the reality of Hollywood today.

How did *Aim* get into this business?

My background was in advertising, I was an account supervisor and a supervisor of media planning at different ad agencies. I really was able to see how clients spend their money and what they get back in return from the traditional media spending. Commercial advertising was always the halcyon of marketing where corporations spent the bulk of their money. Having been supervisor of media planning, dealing with networks and all the fees associated with it, I was in the perfect space to analyze return on investment and how much it takes to get a brand name and product into the consumer psyche.

One agency I worked with was the first company to produce a mini-series. The mini-series concept was produced as original programming for independent stations in the television markets who had to compete with network programming and found it hard to sell their commercial spots against such strong programming when all they had to offer up were reruns. All of this experience gave me the background I needed to begin to explore a new field that was in its infancy; but offered the opportunity to leap frog over traditional marketing and right into the consumer's line of sight. One of the ad agencies I worked for did marketing for film companies. Then I met my current partner, Joyce Phillips, and she was already doing product placement, but not entertainment tie-in promotions, which I had started doing for the studios I worked with. Twenty years ago her company was formed and we became partners eighteen years ago when we expanded to a full service entertainment marketing company.

My partner and I got together and we kept expanding. Of course the pitch to the corporations continually changed because it was an evolving business and there were no textbooks about it and certainly no measurement of what this delivers, which is what corporations want to know, what is the return on the investment?

What is the difference between product placement and branded content?

It is really the same thing. There is an evolution that product placement made over the last twenty years. Products were appearing in films by the natural cause of selection or the creative process and some people were becoming friends with editors and when they saw the product in the films they would think, "Gee this is a great idea. I should just go tell the corporation that I can get their product in this movie and charge them for doing that!" Actually, the product was placed there by a production person in order to satisfy a set need or a prop need, but people began to see the immediate tie in with corporations. So product placement was really meant to be something that lent authenticity to a set or a scene.

The advantage to getting a product placed by design instead of accident is that it also came with the legal clearance necessary to permit its use. It became a legitimate business when it became a legal practice to authorize the use of a product. With this came the inherent desire by each and every brand to have their product and brand name protected from inappropriate use as well. When you are working on the film the reality is that if you want the viewer to feel like they're immersed in this storytelling, you want the environment to be as familiar to the viewer as possible.

We are a branded nation so the brand names lend authenticity to a character and/or to a set. Product Placement agencies actually began popping up to be the intermediary between the studios and the corporations working in the best interests of both; providing the product and also protecting the brand from any placements deemed to be in bad taste or damaging to the brand name. Then it became competitive, because when you've got a placement like *Coca-Cola* in the hands of a major actor and *Pepsi* saw it, of course *Pepsi* wanted to be there and then other soft drinks began vying for the same opportunities. It had the instant ability of making a brand "cool," "hip," and "relevant."

The business sprung up really just to service productions and in the process all of us at young agencies realized it was a money making proposition. Every agency basically created their own models. What we knew we needed to do of course was represent corporations and service productions and during this process make a lot of friends along the way who would facilitate the process: producers, directors, writers, and production people.

A major contribution that we make is that we facilitate the legal clearances for the use of brand name product for the studios, but it is really the producers who benefit from the work we do because through the loan of product we defray their production costs. There are a lot of young filmmakers who come to me and ask *AIM* for funding. A lot of these independent films can be made on a shoestring. Their entire budget may only be from $25,000 to $75,000.

Because product placement has taken a major spotlight roll in feature film marketing, most independent filmmakers who are just coming up see the major films with these large product placements, and they assume those corporations are financing that film.

That is not the case. Generally, they are simply defraying costs by contributing product that would otherwise have to be purchased or rented, and with the fee placements they are securing exclusivity for their brands. With both types of commitments, if it is substantial enough-the value of the loaned goods, or the fee paid-they may receive guarantees from the studio that the product will be featured. The value to the marketer is that their product has the chance of high visibility in a feature film with worldwide distribution.

They are defraying costs.

Yes, they even use a product placement in a major picture, like a Tom Cruise film—*Minority Report* for instance. Event films of this type do have placement fees for participation that normally can start at $250,000. When you are talking about a film like *Minority Report* and you add all those placements up it comes to 1 to 2 million dollars worth of placement and it is only a tiny dent in the budget of that film. So while $250,000 would be a windfall for an independent film, it is a token fee for exclusivity on a film of this size. And on the flip side, a smaller film could not ask for $250,000 for a placement because those fees would only be considered by a company if it is an A-List blockbuster film with a an A-List actor.

On a smaller scale with a smaller film, these filmmakers will come to me and say, "We have this great opportunity and I can take a product like *Snapple* and the whole story can be about *Snapple* and we are only asking for $12,000."

Our clients are spoiled; they are not used to paying for placements when they don't have to.

Because I have a soft spot for these young filmmakers I tell them, "I will get you goods and services to keep your costs down and help you with crafts services, which I don't do for large films." However on a small independent film I will sometimes provide product for craft services because every donation helps.

What do you ask for in return for these donations to independentfilmmakers?

If I give them beverages and food products, things that you can use for craft services, I will ask them to place the products in the film as well and provide me with a finished copy of the film. I may be able to get them locations for nothing, or I may be able to hook them up with wardrobe or with electronics, or if they need a gym, or exercise equipment. These are all things they would have to put into the budget below the line for sets or props. They always appreciate any assistance I can provide. They must promise me however that they won't forget who was there for them when they started-when they hit it big! I'm always rooting for them.

I can tell you this is a hard sell for me to sell corporations on these independent films because they want to be in the films that have wide distribution and yet I can tell you that more than five of the top ten films at Sundance in 2003 are the films that I helped. In fact some of my clients came back and said "*AIM* productions and Patti Ganguzza's names were all over the place!" I think that is great. I didn't ask for credits but they gave them freely.

Even *Hebrew Hammer* was so grateful for whatever I gave them and this is a pleasure to me because I think that the little independents need my help more than the large films.

Do people who are looking for product placement need to send you a script first?

Every single project starts with a synopsis so I can take a look and see if the content is something I would consider working on. It is impossible for me to get product into an "R-rated" film that is full of sex and violence. Remember these are companies that have spent millions of dollars to create a brand image and you can kill it in an instant with a bad placement.

The synopsis is my first glance then I read the entire script and do my own breakdown scene-by-scene, set-by-set. On a studio property I will provide them with a complete list of what I can provide the production with and which placement opportunities are of keen interest to me for one or more of my brands. From there on it is a negotiating proposition with the studios. Smaller independents, as I said, work differently.

There is a responsibility that we take on and there is a responsibility on the filmmaker to insure that there is not anything damaging or disparaging to a brand. Some films I will give them the product for craft services and I will say, "I can help you with your costs, but please don't place the product in the film anywhere." It is just basically a gift.

On the reverse side if it is a great little film, then I want to see the product used in a manner where I would see the brand name in at least one scene. It doesn't have to be seen more than once to satisfy my placement requirements.

Can independent filmmakers get cash for their films from corporations?

Usually if an independent filmmaker comes to me and they have credentials then I might be able to get a small fee for them, but generally speaking the ones that call me are new directors.

151

For example when *Hebrew Hammer* came to me they didn't have any credentials for me to sell them so I basically gave permission and I gave them product to use from my clients because I thought it was a good project.

I didn't get my clients too involved in it because in my primary contract with my client I have the authority to place their product wherever I see fit, so I didn't really enlist them to say, "Oh, you should really do this film and if you really like it, maybe give him some money to promote it at Sundance." I didn't do this because they would want to know why I was recommending this film when these producers did not have any credentials. Now, this producer has credentials and that I *can* talk about to my clients.

Is it easier to get corporations into films with celebrities?

We also worked on *Pieces of April*, which had some celebrities in it. I love the independents. I can certainly say that in some instances I can assist them with funding on a small level but not on a level where a corporation would put up the money to actually produce the film, because my clients are not in the business of film financing, and if they were they would have a better way to measure a film as an investment. Everything in the corporate world is measuring return on their investment. The film business is very risky and [independent films do not] fit their business model.

Do you find product placement for documentaries?

I have had a lot of discussions with documentary filmmakers and I always tell them to bring the project because this is different. If this is a documentary that will be on a cable network that has a very targeted audience then maybe my corporate clients would be interested in sponsorship. Often we can negotiate a deal with the producer before they partner with a distributor and the partnership adds to the desirability of the property when securing their distribution deals, because there is so much of this out there. It is a tricky proposition though and we have to be careful what we commit to.

Sponsorship money is very different than some of the independent films that come to us and ask for finance. Sponsorship money means that we want to associate the brand's name and product with the film property because we think its theme and interest will appeal to some of our consumers.

A documentary comes with credibility about a particular topic that our clients have found out through personality profiles on their consumers that a particular field or topic interests them. For instance someone who does a documentary on Hollywood legends might be of interest to *Revlon*, or *Max Factor*. Then I would help them get some funding from *Revlon* to put into the film and use it as a sponsorship.

The producers can use this money any way they want. I would negotiate an end-credit with a full screen, "Special thanks for *Revlon*," and also a lead-in when it airs. It would have to say, "This program is brought to you by *Revlon*." Sponsorship dollars you can make a case for because it will air on TV and *Revlon* will get their opening billboard, their closing billboard and the voice over with "Sponsorship brought to you by . . ." This has immediate value to *Revlon* if the show appeals to a clearly target consumer segment.

What other ways are sponsorship dollars spent?

There are many opportunities for sponsorships, integrated product placement, and promotional tie-ins with primetime TV shows, specials, reality series and such. Fox Sports has been very active in this area and has been most creative in their ideas and execution. For example, *The Best*

153

Damn Sports Show. Our clients came in as sponsor of the show and the product placement became part of the deal that we made with them for fully integrated use of the product brand name. There was a commercial commitment as well to secure this.

The structure of these deals usually involves the media commitment. If it is a series for instance, one commercial spot per episode would be the minimum required. In addition to the media dollars, a separate fee is usually charged for the integration of the product within the show. Product is woven into the production through the use of branded segments, product usage, or logo branding somewhere on the set. For *Fear Factor*, for instance, a brand logo can appear on a time clock. For *American Idol*, the branding on set is delivered with the *Coke* glasses that sit in front of each judge. In all cases the media commitment is predicated on the desire for guaranteed product placement with the series. Not random, but carefully planned.

You do this from looking at the script and knowing where it will be broadcast?

When sponsorship dollars are committed, the sponsor takes a more active role in the creative decisions that will determine how and where their branding, product, and message will be integrated into the show or series. There are no hard and fast rules. Each show will present different opportunities. If we are talking about a skateboarding competition, all we could do would be to show some signage along the skateboarding route. If we follow the model of sports, sponsor branding is seen in some of the most unexpected places.

When you see the players come off the court and they have *Gatorade* cups in their hands and *Nike* towels around their necks and the guys are wearing *Motorola* headphones, it is all branding. No one tells them they have to hold the cup a certain way or turn their head to camera so we can see the logo. [The logo captures] us when we least expect it because we are so absorbed in the game. That is what we look for: integration that is organic and placed in a way that it doesn't interrupt the viewing pleasure.

So branded content is really from my point of view, a more dedicated integration of the product. Branded content takes on more of the definition of sponsorship vis-a-vi there are dollars committed beyond placing the product in the show.

For instance look at what *Revlon* did with *All My Children*. The whole storyline evolved around a small business being threatened by a larger company like *Revlon*. It was all a branded content deal that became a fully integrated sponsorship. There was a physical product on the show. There were verbal mentions that were fully integrated into the story line and this become better branded content than if you just placed the product in someone's hands or on their sets.

Would you say there are two levels of Branding?

Absolutely. And yet there is still good value in the passive ones. If I put cereal in someone's kitchen on a primetime TV show, once I've established that this is the cereal that this family eats, for continuity purposes it will always be somewhere on that kitchen set for the life of that season. While it may not be the level of exposure equivalent to branded content visibility, you do get those impressions week-to-week and slowly it builds up an awareness of the brand associated with that character or the show.

Standard product placement in TV is not as accepted by the networks because they feel it might interrupt some bigger deals on the horizon. Networks have begun testing the waters of product integration with their reality series and with promotional integration that comes with a sponsor's tie-in promotion to launch a new season or highly promoted special episode. In Europe and abroad however, product placement in television series is common practice because they don't produce many films over there so the value of product placement is heavily focused in TV shows.

You mean those product placements we saw in *Seinfeld* weren't paid for?

No, I represented those companies. We placed the *Snapple* in there, we placed the *Post* cereals, we placed the *Stairmaster* in all of those episodes. Every time there was a gym seen in that series we would mobilize $75,000 to $100,000 worth of product and get it over to the set. We would make that gym look as authentic as possible. The scene would be shot and we would ship it right back to our storage. If they had to rent that equipment it would cost them thousands of dollars to do that. I would get it there on our own dime and give it to them for their use at no cost.

We always start by being a production resource for the television productions and feature films we assist. When *Seinfeld* needed east coast seaweed for an episode, we found it. This was the episode where Kramer was practicing his golf swing at the beach.

In terms of goods and services, anything they ever needed I would make sure we found it. I had to call all over the state of Maine to find a company willing to ship over a barrel of east coast seaweed for them to make that beach scene look authentic. I didn't even know there was a difference between East and West coast seaweed at the time! I found a willing partner up in Maine to ship it for me.

On *Seinfeld*, the writers were always writing brand names into the scripts but even though they wrote it into the script, it was my responsibility to get companies to agree to it. Not every company thinks something scripted is funny, especially if they are talking about their brand.

A simple answer to your question is no, they did not pay to be on *Seinfeld*. This is the one show that brought product placement to light because the writers were just so brand friendly. Even though the networks were constantly telling the producers, "You can't do this," every week the producers were like, "Hey, we are your number one show. Are you really going to tell us that we can't do this?"

The producers had all of the power because they had a hit on their hands. Most new unproven shows don't have that much confidence to defy the networks because doing so might get them kicked off the network.

We do a lot for productions, sometimes on their request, sometimes on our suggestion. For instance, when *Real World* first started, I was the one who negotiated the Ikea deal for their show. I was talking to the producers and I found out that every series is a different house in a different city. One day I was talking to the producer who said, "I have to furnish this house." And I said, "Why don't we just get a furniture sponsor, then you don't have to go buying furniture every time you go to a new house?"

I pitched the idea to *Ikea* and they loved the association with this show. I negotiated the end-credit with the full logos saying, "Furnishings provided by *Ikea*." Even though it wasn't an *MTV* produced show it ended up airing on *MTV* and if *MTV* had been the producers I would never have gotten away with that. *MTV* would have put a big dollar value on that. We did this deal on barter. Ikea completely furnished every house for every *Real World* from that point forward. The deal has never changed.

How did AIM get compensated for this?

We didn't! *Ikea* was not a client of mine at the time. I just cold called them and pitched the idea. Never underestimate the power of the pitch! It was a great way for me to establish our credibility with the producers and strengthened our leverage with them.

I talk to corporations every day about brands and you need to know about how brand marketing works to be able to sell them on an idea. You have to know what excites them and what doesn't. You have to know what they are willing to pay for and what they are not. I read a script a day just for feature films and we work on every primetime television show as well—network and cable.

The film scripts I read are all films in production that were picked up by major studios. Of course in-between the studio properties I am reading independents that we regularly help. I am just a big fan of independents. When you watch the Academy Awards, nine out of ten of those awards go to the independents because it is the best work.

We are educating our brands and corporations on getting more involved in the support of film because film entertains and communicates in a way that nothing else can. Each involvement however must be analyzed so they see their return on the investment. We can no longer simply sell the sizzle, we must deliver the steak.

Do you have any stories you can tell about documentaries that you have helped with branding?

We worked with this man who is an official explorer for *Discovery*. He has had many articles written about him in the science section of the *New York Times* about his deep-sea dives. He was the one who was diving for one of Columbus's ships and they did a documentary on it. He called me and told me how much computers are a part of his work. He said they have special software and they map everything out and all of the findings are logged back into the computer. I represented *Gateway Computers* at the time, so I said I would be interested in giving him a *Gateway* computer if he can in some part of the documentary show

how the computer assists him in this very interesting process of discovery. We would love this and I would encourage *Gateway* to participate.

We gave him a laptop, which he was so grateful for. In this instance his show was already picked up and financed by *Discovery.* It is not the distributor's job to take care of your production needs like goods and services that companies like *AIM* provide.

These kinds of things actually excite my clients because they are great PR stories. They may not get a lot of product placement visibility but they get PR and that is very important to corporations.

Tell us what the corporations want from producers.

We don't ask them to force anything that would not normally occur in their story telling, because I don't believe that anyone in the product placement world should be forcing creative. I believe that anything that we do for the corporations, which also is at the end of the day what studios want, is to have your product placed in a very organic and relevant way so that the character that is drinking the beverage is relevant to the character and is also relevant to the brand, meaning that this is typically a person who would drink this beverage.

I never force product placement anywhere. I think that the best we can hope for is that we establish the brand as a desirable product. For example in the documentary we had a *Gateway* computer in the hands of this incredible explorer who relies on his computer to document his findings. That is a great PR story because we want people to take *Gateway Computers* seriously.

When I place it in TV shows basically I am not looking for the celebrity profile with the lead of the show, but with a documentary, it is another situation. He will give me an end-credit saying, Computers supplied by *Gateway*," or,

159

"Special thanks to *Gateway Computers*." Any time that he is being interviewed he can mention it. I gave him some ideas and brand attributes that will make the client happy to hear.

For instance, someone doing a documentary that ended up on *Black History Month*, we have a lot of clients who are looking for ethnic consumer marketing. If we were sure that the subject of the documentary was uplifting and complimented the brand strategy, and someone came to me several months before *Black History Month*, we could potentially find the client who would be willing to sponsor that show.

The way media works in this country is that if you sold your show to the distributor, the distributor needs to make their money back through the commercials they sell. If the producers make a deal upfront prior to closing their distribution deal they usually hold back a few commercial spots for the corporate sponsor they bring in from their end. You can bring the program in as sponsored programming before you hand it over to the networks.

Let's say this documentary gets a company to sponsor their show, in exchange for the sponsorship dollars, the producer gives the corporation a minimum of two or three commercial spots in the show, and usually a voice over, "Brought to you by . . .", then they hand it off to the distribution channel hopefully with one sponsor already in place. This will not interrupt the sales initiative of the people at that network who have to sell the commercial spots; but it will lock out competitors in that category.

Then of course the sponsor gets the opening billboard and the two or three commercial spots without having to buy them from *Discovery Channel*, from *A&E*, from the *Learning Channel*, etc. This is sponsored programming.

The producers can negotiate these deals and the deals they negotiate with the cable network is, "We will give you this show complete but we want to hold back two of the commercial spots." Generally speaking in a half-hour you have 22 spots so they have 20 more commercials left to sell.

You need to make the deals when you go to the network and expect that you can sell your spots.

When you go to the distributor he wants to sell all of the spots so you need to get the spots in the deals you cut at the beginning.

Tell us what types of products you can get for producers.

We represent the entire *Unilever Corporation*; one of the deodorants, maybe a deodorant for an action show or a personal care product; female product like *Ponds* or *Dove* on a show about women. As long as we know there is a distribution in place for the television special or film, we can sell the sponsorship concept on those documentaries.

The advertiser gives the company a chance to see something before it hits the sales department and generally speaking we could always sell them on the idea that they are getting a deal because it is coming directly from the producer.

For instance, *American Idol*; we worked directly with the producer from London. Once it became a hit on *Fox* then every meeting *Fox* had to be present and the producers had to be present because *Fox* placed different restrictions on the deal making. Once the network comes in, the price tag goes up.

If the producers can bring the program through a distributor and say, "I have *Dove* interested in sponsoring part of my program," then the distributor sees a bigger value in the property. The likelihood is that the channel distributor will have an easier time selling the rest of the spots.

161

Generally speaking I am always asking, "Who are you speaking to? Do you have a distribution deal?" It would be very hard for our clients to put up money for a show that gets produced and never gets aired. There was a show like that called *No Boundaries* that *Ford* put up half of the money to produce this show and the show never got picked up. Now they are looking for ways to distribute the show through video and other distribution, so *Ford* can at least get back some kind of impression for the money they spent.

I heard that there were three levels of branding with *Ford*. One is where they will come in with a car if they like your script, the second is when they give you all the cars for the film, and the third is when they give you all the cars and some money for the film too. How does this work?

It is based on the project, the deal, and who's selling it. In a feature film they might provide the cars and pay a fee as well if the placement in the film is a featured one. In a show like *No Boundaries* where they feel from a company point of view they can take that whole *No Boundaries* concept into the market place and really use the *No Boundaries* theme and build a consumer campaign off of it, they paid for the rights to do that.

Just giving cars doesn't grant a company the licensing rights. The title *No Boundaries* was perfect, the theme was perfect, so they helped finance the property in exchange for those licensing rights as well. If I place a product in *Will & Grace*, my marketer doesn't have the rights to use *Will & Grace* in the market place just because they have a product in the show. I would have to go back to NBC to say, "What would it cost for us to do a *Will & Grace* Promotion?"

I went to a studio once to do a tie-in with a hit series they produced and they told me, "This will cost you a million dollars and 16% royalty on everything you sell." I said,

"We're not looking for a license. I just want to do an in-store promotion around the show." Because the show had already become a hit series, the studio would not permit a tie-in promotion without a licensing fee.

Although I always tell people there are no rules, you have to keep in mind what will excite the corporation about the project. Because if it makes sense, and if there is a distribution and it fits a particular consumer profile, it will have a perceived value.

There are some natural tie-ins. Some people are doing documentaries and let's say they are doing a film on plastic surgery and there is one big face cream that everyone uses after plastic surgery, then this may have a value to this manufacturing company to be in this documentary. What would you charge them? You have to find out what are your costs. What kind of returns would you like? What are you willing to give up for the amount of money you are asking?

I always say that financing is the most creative part of the development of any film or entertainment project. Most people think it's the story. I maintain it's the financing because without financing, no story can be told.

When I started teaching a class at NYU film school, I realized these students come to this school at great expense, with a great time commitment, and it is the only degree at this level that doesn't guarantee you a job upon graduation. Each year they have to produce a student film that will cost them $25,000 to make. It is mind-boggling. You have to have a passion in order to pursue this career. That passion which stems from a 'state of mind' must carry through and work in every part of your development. That's why I always tell the students, "Don't think in the total number of $25,000, think of the ways you can chip away at the $25,000.

I tell them to do the math and see how much real dollars you need, and how much can be defrayed with donations. You must go to every resource you can think of because the more people you talk to and the more sources you go to the more you understand how this business works. One of the ways to get people to part with their money is to be able to communicate your vision to them.

Your pitch is very important to your film. I am on the phone every single day. I cold call every body. Granted I represent 200 brand name companies but when I am servicing a production I am calling everybody. It is very hard to get corporations to part with their money. You have to give them a reason and you need to understand who you are talking to. My dad used to say, "Remember before whom you are speaking."

You need to understand that the pitch for a corporation may not be the same pitch for someone who wants to get into the film business. You should just use your passion about your film to get them to take their savings and give it to you to be a producer. There are many people who want to be in the film business and they don't have a clue on how to get a return on their money, but they want to be in the film business. Then you just want to be honest and let them know the passion you are communicating is the passion you will deliver in the film. Anyone who invests at this level knows they are investing in you, not the film. There are people who want to get into the film business and they will buy their way in.

There may be people you would never think of asking: a cousin, an uncle, someone you meet at *Starbucks*. Just never lose the passion for your film. I know two young men who were going to school to become filmmakers who now have a deal for a feature film. Their story is amazing. They are two guys from NYU who wanted to be filmmakers and in order to support themselves through school they started filming weddings, one right after the other, to make the money to produce the school films. By the time they finished school they figured the best story they had was the story they created! They wrote a story about themselves on how they had to film weddings to get through film school and now a studio has picked up this film and thinks that it is a funny script.

Filmmakers and documentary filmmakers have a passion about what they do, but what they don't have is a business head. That is the only thing they are missing. The business head thinks, "How do I manifest the money? Where do I manifest the money?"

When filmmakers call me to ask, "Will *Snapple* give me $12,000 to make this film?" I say, "No, but let's talk about this film and look for ways to tackle this budget." I tell filmmakers to go to their local stores for help as most of them would love to be part of a film. Go to the businesses you frequent, and the people you know. Go to the places you shop. Get to know the owners of those businesses and talk about what you love to do.

The way you think creatively about your project is the way you have to think creatively about your financing.

Pattie, you have so much information to give to filmmakers I am really glad you are teaching.

I think NYU has such a unique group of young filmmakers it is a joy to teach there. I love to work with the independents. I am the president of the company and I take care of them myself.

Just remember goods translates into dollars. Every time you have to go out and buy lunch for someone—a bottle of soda, rent a light, rent a cell phone—you may be able to get these things donated and that can save you money on the bottom line.

The way you think creatively about your project is the way you have to think creatively about your financing. Remember, you are in the *business* of film. It *is* a business.

I don't wait for moods. You accomplish nothing if you do that. Your mind must know it has got to get down to earth.

—Pearl S. Buck

PUBLIC TELEVISION

The Money Maze of Public Funding: Working With ITVS & PBS

I always feel like I'm in the middle of a *Monty Python* movie when I try to find information on those public television web sites. I can see John Cleese with that comedic expression on his face looking totally baffled by all of it. Fortunately Patric Hedlund wrote *A Breadcrumb Trail Through the PBS Jungle: The Producer's Survival Guide*, and created a map to the public television system. This book is an essential field manual for producers, complete with a Secret Acronym Decoder! You can pick up a copy of Patric's book at http://www.forests.com/breadcrumb.

Remember, there is some money here for you but you need to know how to carefully tread the path and get out of the maze before dark!

When President Johnson signed the Public Broadcasting Act in 1967, he said the creation of public broadcasting would ". . . give a wider . . . stronger voice to educational radio and television by providing new funds for broadcast facilities."

The Corporation for Public Broadcasting (CPB) provides the largest source of funding for Public Television. PBS is not a network. It is a private, nonprofit membership organization that funds and distributes programs for more than 340 member stations located throughout the United States. Programs that air on PBS are produced through member stations and the independent film community.

PBS has access to three funds: the General Program Fund, which typically funds programming for major mini-series; the PBS/CPB Challenge Fund, which is designated toward co-producing major mini series where significant funds are allocated for one-hour programming (these projects must be approved by both PBS and the CPB); and the Carlton fund, managed by the CPB, and Carlton Television International, which is available for projects that appeal to a worldwide audience and are distributed internationally.

By the mid 1980's complaints that the CPB had failed to diversify programming and give a voice to the unheard minorities were at an all time high. In 1988 Congress passed a new federal mandate challenging the CPB to negotiate with a national coalition of independent producer groups to establish a truly independent television service and in 1991 the Independent Television Service (ITVS) was born.

Producing for Public Broadcasting

PBS

The focus at PBS is on their returning strands and their icon series, with less focus on limited series programming, and even less on single documentary programming. While PBS does schedule one-off programming, 80% of their schedule is reserved for the major multi-part series (strands), which typically run four to six episodes. The strands also command the greater part of the PBS budget.

There is an up side and a down side to working with PBS. When you bring PBS a program with a $1 million dollar budget it will end up coming in at $1.5 million because of all of the required ancillary elements. This includes all of the activities surrounding promotion and advertising, such as on-air promos and the development and maintenance of a website, as well as those activities that are integral to PBS's philosophy, such as educational programs, audience outreach, and closed captioning. These expenses must be covered in addition to normal production expenses, so if you're going to produce with PBS, you must raise extra funds. The good news is PBS raises funds too.

Even projects that receive significant funding from PBS usually only end up with one-fourth to one-third of the production budget, which means producers working with PBS are usually required to seek additional funding from outside sources. The program producer is also responsible for managing all aspects of a project's development and production. PBS will consider allocating finishing funds for one-off programs, though they usually do not make that decision until a project has reached the rough-cut stage of production.

PBS Children's programming has a significant infrastructure with anywhere from 10 to 20 million dollars raised for weekday programs. These multi-million dollar productions typically run about 45 episodes per season, which places children programming beyond the scope of most independent filmmakers.

PBS accepts proposals on an ongoing basis. Proposals are evaluated according to the quality of the proposal, the credentials of the production team, PBS's schedule needs, and the financial commitment required by PBS. PBS wants quality programs that are journalisticly sound and will reach a broad spectrum of people. If you have a project in mind, you need to make sure that your project is in sync with PBS's goals for your particular target audience.

If your proposal meets the PBS criteria it is forwarded to the senior director for the appropriate genre, who will present your proposal to a content team. Together they will evaluate your proposal and make specific recommendations regarding your project. Your funding plan and your list of possible donors will be forwarded to PBS's underwriting department so that each of your potential funding sources can be verified as an acceptable donor. The senior programming team then reviews recommended proposals and makes the final decision on whether or not to green light the project. This team includes PBS's president and CEO and PBS programming executives in Virginia, Florida and California.

There are other ways of getting on PBS. Some producers distribute their films on a market-by-market situation by contacting each PBS station. PBS Plus feeds programs to local stations to be picked up and scheduled on an ala carte basis. These programs are completely underwritten so they come to PBS fully funded. Producers should also consider other funding sources available for PBS through ITVS and the CPB Minority Consortia, which covers contemporary issues that fall within the five minority consortia including: Latino Public Broadcasting, National Black Programming Consortium, Native American Telecommunications Association, the National Asian American Telecommunications Association, and the Pacific Islands Telecommunications Association.

If you are even thinking about producing for public television you need to visit the respective web site and carefully review their guidelines. They have very strict guidelines on who can underwrite programs and if they feel even one of your underwriters has any real or perceived influence regarding the content of your project they will not accept it.

American Public Television (APT)

APT is the main distributor for thousands of quality series and single programs in all genres, including: children's, drama, performance, comedy, music, documentaries, news and public affairs, and how-to series. They offer a wide array of marketing and distribution services and will provide promotion and ongoing carriage reports for a fee.

APT works with all 349 public television stations to help shape content, program design and pledge formats. APT has developed some of the most successful public television funding-raising programs, such as: The Moody Blues in Concert at the Red Rocks, and the Dr. Andrew Weil specials.

ITVS

ITVS was designed to open the door to independent producers by acting as a bridge between producers and public television. They are interested in subject matters that may be controversial and would not have been funded without their support.

Programs that air on ITVS are utilized beyond the initial broadcast, through the public education system and various public programs designed to stimulate group discussions. They want films that will promote healthy dialogue; therefore, the ITVS judges will consider your film's potential for promoting stimulating conversation as one of the most important criteria during the evaluation process.

ITVS encourages emerging producers to bring their projects. While they do not sponsor student works, they are looking for individuals who want to be professionals. ITVS will embrace filmmakers who are just on the doorstep, and will accept the responsibility of nurturing emerging filmmakers as they make their way into the industry.

ITVS will be involved throughout your entire project as your executive producer. This is a full service organization. Services include funding, creative development, feedback during production, and a comprehensive public television launch which includes marketing, publicity, website, station relations and outreach support. They have thirteen grassroots staff members who take new projects around the country into local communities where they work on building an audience.

They have two open calls a year, with deadlines on February 25 and August 15 of each year. It takes judges about four months during each round to read and evaluate submitted proposals. One recent round included 640 proposals. The rounds operate in either two stages or three stages. Usually there is an internal cut followed by a second phase, then the third phase, which goes to a panel.

During the reapplication stage, filmmakers who are selected for the last round will have an opportunity to address certain issues brought up by the judging panel. Filmmakers submit a detailed budget during this reapplication period. The panel will discuss and evaluate each proposal before deciding which ones will be considered for funding.

The most crucial phase in the selection process is the Orientation. During this phase, producers whose projects have been selected so far travel to San Francisco where they will undergo two and a half days of intense meetings filled with essential information about ITVS's role during production.

ITVS also features *Links*, a joint proposal between producers and local public television stations that provide matching production funds. *Links* is considered a very important project because it promotes the collaborative effort and allows projects to reach smaller stations that do not have a competitive edge.

When ITVS funds a project they require a licensing fee for US broadcast. This license gives them copyright over the project during the duration of broadcasting, which usually covers six releases in four years, or four releases in three years, after which all rights revert back to the producer. The producer will control the international rights, home video rights, domestic and international rights, educational domestic rights, and the international theatrical domestic rights while ITVS will enjoy domestic rights for television broadcast.

If ITVS is the full funder they will take 50% of the royalties of other funding, this is their back-end share for the funding they put in, which can be considerable compared to what is available. Some of this funding comes from the

Corporation for Public Broadcasting (CPB), which is ITVS's funder. There is a back-end share of revenues earned, which is put back in the production fund for future funding of other projects. If ITVS puts in 100% of the budget, they get a 50% return, if they put in 50% of the budget, they get a 25% return. They get 50% return for whatever percent they put into the budget.

ITVS participates in foreign coproduction partnerships with *ZDF Germany*, *ARTE France*, the *BBC*, and many other international distributors. This partnership allows several organizations to share the responsibility of funding, and creates a wider distribution base for films, which encourages more production.

If ITVS offers something to NPS and they turn it down they can offer it to PBS Plus. PBS Plus does not have national carriage and you can work with the individual stations. They also work with strands (such as *Frontline*), which have timeslots that can accommodate additional programs. ITVS will also take programs to presenting stations such as *Nebraska Educational Telecommunications* (NET), or *Oregon Public Broadcasting* (OPB). If these options do not workout, ITVS will send the program out via satellite and will send notification out to local stations letting them know when they can download the program. These stations can then air the program according to their scheduling needs. Sometimes if you work station by station you can get as much coverage as a national broadcast.

ITVS has additional calls on a year-to-year basis that address specific topics that may emerge throughout the year. For example, they commissioned thirty producers to do a one-minute piece on the aftermath of 9/11. When digital technology exploded onto the film scene, ITVS put out a special call for programs produced on DV. ITVS wanted to explore the different ways this technology would impact the industry and they encouraged filmmakers to submit applications for their DV projects. Keep watching the ITVS web site for these types of calls.

ITVS, INDEPENDENT LENS

Independent Lens started out as a series of ten docs that previously aired on PBS for about three seasons. In 2003 they established a 29-week national PBS series that showcases independent documentaries, dramas, experimental films, and shorts. *Independent Lens* is a partnership between ITVS and PBS that is designed to give independent programs a year-round presence on PBS, and is part of the program service ITVS provides to the stations. They fully expect that a large number of programs that ITVS chooses to fund will be a part of this series, and hope to use this series to showcase work that is distinctive in content. This is good news for all documentary filmmakers.

Independent Lens wants programs that are "innovative, provocative, character driven, and well-crafted." Most programs are scheduled in one-hour time slots.

WNET And *Wide Angle*

Thirteen WNET is New York's PBS flagship station. Stephen Segaller is the Director of News and Public Affairs; Bill Grant is in charge of the Sciences, Natural History and Features departments; and Jack Bender is in charge of Arts and Culture. Each department features one or more strands that are the core of PBS programming.

The news department at WNET launched *Wide Angle*, a weekly series of one-hour international documentaries that recently filled the time slot vacated by *Frontline*. *Wide Angle* just completed its first season and producers are confident they will be back next year for anther run.

Segaller rarely looks at single documentaries for *Wide Angle* unless they have a solid international or current affairs appeal. If he receives a proposal that has a good science spin, or might be good material for *Frontline* he will send the proposal off to the respective producers of these programs.

Because WNET is based in New York, they are the most watched station in the public broadcasting system. This puts them in a very strong position at the international markets when producers are searching for foreign distribution and foreign coproduction deals.

Program producers at WNET have only included six or seven single one-hour or 90-minute docs in the last two years. They occasionally acquire individual programs for the New York City market; however, this is not a place to find significant funding, as the acquisition prices are in the low few thousands of dollars. They encourage producers to bring projects with some funding already attached.

Visit www.thirteen.org for additional information on submission guidelines and how to pitch to WNET program producers.

Oren Jacoby

Oren Jacoby of *Storyville Films* made it through the PBS maze with *Topdog Diaries*, a documentary that follows playwright Suzan-Lori Parks during the creation and production of her hit play, *Topdog/Underdog*. According to Oren, "when you are accepted you are told that your film will find a place in the public television system."

Topdog Diaries was lucky enough to find its way on the PBS national schedule through *Stage on Screen*, one of WNET's strand projects.

The story of how Oren got his film on national television is one of perseverance, determination, and instinct. Part of Oren's success story involves ITVS's belief in his cinéma vérté style film; however, like many other documentary filmmakers who start out without a broadcasting

175

station and end up with one, Oren made his share of good luck along the way.

ITVS had never really funded money for development before. But as luck would have it, when Oren called ITVS to pitch his idea, he reached David Liu, the executive in charge of program development at ITVS. Oren wanted to tell a story that would show the playwright's process of bringing words to life. When David heard Oren's pitch he believed in the story and gave him some seed money.

When Oren set out to find a central character he started at the Eugene O'Neill workshop. After sitting through twenty plays he still did not find what he was looking for. Then someone told him about a new writer named Suzan-Lori Parks. He read her script for *Topdog/Underdog* and approached her with the idea of documenting her journey as she went through the creative process of producing her play. Parks agreed and that is when WNET came into the picture.

Suzan Lori-Parks was a great character from the very first day of filming. Her play was good, but there was something else about her that made Oren really sit up and take notice. His original idea was to produce a documentary that would concentrate on several different playwrights, but his instincts told him to concentrate on Parks. If he was going to be true to his original idea of showing the creative process of a playwright, Oren knew that he would have to stick with one writer and get inside this writer's head. He went to David Liu and explained what he wanted to do and Liu encouraged him to follow his instincts.

Up until this time Suzan-Lori Parks was relatively unknown, but true to Oren's instincts she managed to pull-off a successful off-Broadway run, followed by an extended Broadway run, and eventually took the 2002 Pulitzer Prize for Drama.

David Liu must be a wonderful person to work with. He certainly supported Oren through this entire process, and because of his faith in Oren and his project they created a great documentary. There are wonderful people behind ITVS and PBS. Just know they are there to help you create.

Now you know why I want you to perfect your pitch so you can pitch your ideas to anyone, anywhere, at anytime. Oren called ITVS and when David answered the phone he pitched his idea immediately. It must have been a good succinct pitch for David to follow up with Oren and eventually fund him. You may have only 3 to 5 minutes to make your pitch and answer any questions about your film so you must always be prepared for any chance meeting.

Arthur Dong

Arthur Dong is one of the most well respected documentary filmmakers in the industry today. He is a graduate of the Film School at San Francisco State University (1982, Summa Cum Laude) and the *American Film Institute's Center for Advanced Film and Television Studies* (Directing Fellow, 1984). He also sits on the Board of Governors of the *Academy of Motion Pictures Arts and Sciences*, representing the Documentary Branch, and the IFP/*Los Angeles* (Independent Features Project) Board of Directors' Executive Committee. Arthur has won numerous film awards, including a George Foster Peabody Award, three Sundance Film Festival awards, an Oscar(r) nomination, and five Emmy nominations.

His newest documentary, *Family Fundamentals*, explores the emotional issues that envelop three conservative Christian families with gay and lesbian children. The film, which was an official selection of the 2002 Sundance Film Festival, "is a deeply personal look at the "cultural wars" over homosexuality that are being fought in families, communities, and the social/political public spheres of our nation."

Throughout production, Arthur collaborated with a diverse panel that included both gay and lesbian advisors

177

and conservative Christian advisors. He challenged members of the panel to engage in healthy dialogue by resisting the temptation to polarize into two opposing groups. This supported one of the major goals of participating foundations, to support projects that involved an extensive community partnership.

Arthur's film got off the ground when he won *In the Works*, a grant sponsored by *Kodak* and P.O.V./*American Documentary*, Inc. The grant, which offered $10,000 in products, services, or cash, supplied Arthur with the resources to start shooting. With this win under his belt, he forged ahead embracing a proactive strategy for funding. He completed grant applications, networked, and spent quality time taking one-on-one meetings with potential funders. His strategy worked.

In addition to subsequent finishing funds from *American Documentary*, Inc., primary grants came from the *Guggenheim Fellowship in Filmmaking* and the *Theophilus Foundation*, with additional support from numerous sources, including the *Soros Documentary Fund* (now the *Sundance Documentary Fund*), *Eastman Kodak Company*, *Hugh M. Hefner Foundation*, *National Asian American Telecommunications Association* with funds from the *Corporation for Public Broadcasting*, *Los Angeles Cultural Affairs Department*, *Paul Robeson Fund*, *Unitarian Universalist Funding Program*, *California Arts Council Visual Arts Fellowship*, *Columbia Foundation*, *Lear Family Foundation*, *Durfee Foundation*, *Theophilus Fund*, *Lewy Gay Values Fund*, *Gill Foundation*, and the *Jay Cohen Philanthropic Fund of the Horizons Foundation*.

Arthur's final budget for the project came in under $200,000. Funding took about two years from the onset of his original concept to its premier at *Sundance*. He decided early on that the project would be formatted for an arthouse theatrical release alongside a campus college tour, feeling confident that even a tour's limited distribution could generate much needed revenue.

P.O.V. was instrumental in helping Arthur complete his film. They responded to Arthur because he is a filmmaker who steps out and tackles complex issues that encourage communication between diverse groups. Executive Director of P.O.V./*American Documentary*, Cara Mertes, describes Arthur as the kind of filmmaker who, ". . .takes the film out and engages people who don't have a language to talk about their very human experience and how they live that from whatever perspective they are in. We believe this is a great gift." Arthur refuses to preach to the converted.

Arthur kept *Family Fundamental's* production cost down by shooting and editing his own footage and distributing this and his other films through his company, *Deep Focus Productions, Inc.* "This is a good way to build a company," Cara explained, "you are not always waiting for funds to start your project. You can be generating money on your own and paying yourself and your crew back."

Arthur is truly the quintessential solo filmmaker. He did not sit around waiting for his dream to come true. He took control of his own destiny and came up with ideas and strategies that empowered him to create one compelling film after another.

For more information and clips from Arthur's films, please visit his website at www.deepfocusproductions.com.

THE PEACE PRAYER
By Masahisa Goi

May peace prevail on earth
May peace be in our homes and our countries
May our divine missions be accomplished
I thank thee guardian spirits and guardian deities.

GUIDELINES FOR CHANGE

A CONVERSATION WITH
Author, Morrie Warshawski

On Morrie Warshawski's web site he describes himself as a consult-
ant, facilitator and writer. He is being far too modest. Morrie is one of the
best-known film finance gurus in the industry. His list of clients includes
the Corporation for Public Broadcasting, Independent Feature Project,
the John D. and Catherine T. MacArthur Foundation, *the* California
Arts Council, *the* St. Louis Art Museum, *and the* New Orleans Video
Access Center. *He is the author of several fundraising books including,*
"The Fundraising Houseparty: How to Get Charitable Donations From
Individuals in a Houseparty Setting," *and* "Shaking the Money Tree:
How to Get Grants and Donations for Film and Video Projects."

Morrie provides individual consultations with film and video makers,
focusing either on long range career planning or on a specific project. The
advice he offers comes from years of hard-earned experience in the
fundraising world. For more information on Morrie Warshawski's con-
sulting services and his books visit his web site at www.warshawski.com.

Morrie, do you believe we will see a major expansion in the art of filmmaking due to the digital camera?

Absolutely, we have already begun to see it. There is no
doubt in my mind and I think you can find the statistics for
it. It is borne out by our anecdotal evidence, by talking to
people in the field. And the fact is, there are more people

using the medium now because it is more accessible. They can get high quality digital cameras at very low cost.

The other important thing to know about the technology is that you can get desktop editing software that you can use on a Mac or a PC that is also fairly inexpensive and you can edit at home. Between those two ends of the spectrum it has just made the availability of doing visual media work on video a lot more affordable.

Do you think this will increase the number of documentaries being made?

It will increase the number of everything. I think we will see more documentaries, shorts, independent features, more experimental work. We will see more of everything. Actually, the accurate way to say this is that more of everything will be made, whether we will see it or not is another question.

Right. Whether they get distributed and shown is another matter. How will the market support more films? Where will they be shown?

Well, they will have a lot of trouble getting this work shown. Distribution, marketing, and exhibition of work have always been a problem for independent filmmakers.

By hook or crook, my experience is that filmmakers get the work done. They find the money, they beg for money, they do without, they bleed, and they almost always find a way to get the work done. What is out of their control and where they can't be so proactive is in making sure the work gets distributed and out into the market place. That's always a hurdle that is incredibly difficult.

What you are seeing is that the number keeps increasing every time we have a new technology. For example, there were two major shifts that happened in our lifetime. One was the advent of home video, and the second the advent of cable that increased the markets. Now you have the advent of the Internet which provides the capability of streaming work. We keep getting more and more venues of possibilities for people to see your work. That is the upside.

The downside is that it costs more to enter all these markets, and it gets harder to get the work out. Also you have the big conglomerates that keep gobbling up the time and space on any kind of avenue for distribution. When cable first started I had filmmakers coming into my office saying we are in heaven now because there will be fifty channels and they will need all new material so they have to come commission us and buy our work and that did not turn out to be true.

Because they bought old films and TV shows to fill up the time.

Yes. And for new product they chose work that was commercial and reached the largest audience at the lowest price. Of course I am being very general. And now because of cable there are a lot more avenues for making and distributing films, but nothing like the possibilities seemed.

You mean that people may see that same possibility with the advent of digital filming? That filmmakers may see the possibility of more products needed for the 24/7 stations, and streaming their film on the internet, get paid for it and deduce there is a larger market waiting for them?

That's right.

When someone has an idea for a film, how to you recommend they test it to see if it will have an audience?

183

I recommend they test the idea by starting at square one. They need to do basic research to see if anything like the film they want to do has already been created. It is surprising how many people don't do that work. This is just as important for someone doing a fiction narrative as it is for documentaries. It is imperative because if this has already been done then no one will fund it.

Once you have this settled, the second thing is to open it up. I think independents are too isolated. I say go out and talk to these kinds of people. One is distributors, people who know the marketplace. They know these works. Find a distributor who specializes in the kind of picture you are making.

Second you want to talk to your potential audience. Ask yourself who are you making this for and then go talk to them. Tell them about the film you want to make and ask, "What do you think about this?" The whole process is just a lot healthier. Otherwise you may end up with a film that no one wants.

What I find is that many times filmmakers are passionate about the project but are not good writers. Do you recommend these people hire someone to write the proposal?

What I recommend is when they create the proposal it must be perfect. So my recommendation is do whatever this takes. If it means having to hire someone, then so be it. Typically filmmakers even if they are not good at writing can find a partner who can help them write, or they can write a rough first draft and get someone who knows about writing to create a final draft. Most of my clients have the capacity to actually create a good proposal on their own with some assistance. Sometimes it just means having someone like me look at the proposal and make suggestions for change. Occasionally if they need it, and especially if they can afford it, having a professional grant writer is fine.

Where do you find good professional grant writers?

The question is really where you find professional grant writers that know about film and video. This can be hard. There are thousands of people in the U.S. who are grant writers, take a look at the Association of Fundraising Professionals, the AFP. Everyone on this list is a professional grant writer and this is a good place to find grant writers.

The whole reason I wrote my book, *Shaking the Money Tree* is that none of them literally know anything about film and why writing a proposal for a film grant is so different than writing any other proposal. You almost have to have been around filmmakers yourself or have done a few of them to begin to understand the process.

How you find those people is more difficult. I think the best way is to go to the media art centers around the country and see who they recommend. They are all listed at the *National Alliance for Media Arts and Culture* at www.namac.org. You can go to the web site and look by state for a media art center near you. All of the media arts centers are members of NAMAC. You can also talk to other filmmakers for names of people who are good at writing grants.

Once filmmakers have their proposal written can they submit them to you for your guidance?

Yes, I have written over 500 grants myself. I stopped writing 2 years ago. With my hourly rate it is too expensive to write for people and it is not interesting anymore!

An effective way to use my time is just send me the grant package. Then with my critiques almost anyone can write a second draft that will be totally effective.

185

I noticed in the chapter headings of the current edition of *Shaking the Money Tree* you have small businesses listed under funding possibilities. Can you elaborate on this?

Yes, I love small businesses because they are easy to tap for support and they are very informal. They are all around you. You are probably no more than a few blocks away from some small business that you can get support from. That is the upside.

The downside is they never give you money. They are a good source for products. For example I worked with a filmmaker/client of mine in Chicago. She told me the story of a project she was doing with students in the neighborhood. They walked around the neighborhood with a one-page description of the project. They asked the local businesses for things they needed for the film that they normally would have had to pay for. They got free meals every day for the crew from *KFC*, *Pizza Hut* and local restaurants. They needed walkie-talkies and they couldn't find them and the local cell phone company let them have unlimited use of five cell phones for a week. For the script, the local Kinko's let them have free photocopies. I tell filmmakers all the time to look through their budgets and pick out things small businesses can donate to you. It is as good as money.

These small businesses are very easy to approach. You just literally walk through the door and ask for the manager and you can talk to them right there. They can make a decision very quickly. What you may give them in return is a credit on the film, or they might want an invitation to the film or a free video copy when it is released.

What about larger corporations? For example, corporations that are yielding between $12 and $20 million a year that may not have an established founda-

tion, but are starting to get involved in the industry, perhaps advertising on PBS?

When you are dealing with a corporation and want to ask them for money then you have to jump through a completely different set of hoops than with a small business. This is much, much harder. Most of my clients have not had much luck with corporations. I would say there are some general things to keep in mind that are true about corporations.

One thing to consider, unlike a private foundation, there is usually more than one door you can go through, and it is not always clear which one you should go through. For instance, one door might be human resources, or another door that is a lot more usual is the marketing door, or the community relations door. There is another door that no one talks about and that is the CEO's door. If the CEO has a personal interest in the topic of the film, or knows someone you know, well then that door might open to you. You need to think of all these doors before you approach the corporation.

Another thing about corporations that is difficult is that if they don't have a formal giving program or foundation it is hard to do the research. They might have given to a film before but it may not be found on the paperwork. Unlike a private foundation that has to list everything, they may have just expensed the money, as they do not have to list it separately. This makes the research difficult.

The basis of all good fundraising is savvy research. So what is a good filmmaker to do? The answer is obvious. You need a personal contact. You almost always need someone who will walk you through one of the doors if you want to get corporate money.

Let's say you decide to go for corporate money. What type of package would you need to take them?

187

That's the other bug-a-boo. A normal grant proposal won't work in a corporation because they never really give you the money outright. If you get a donation from a corporation it is almost always a marketing buy. Filmmakers can call it whatever they want, but to them they are buying something. That means when you go to them you have to talk to them in a way that is very different from talking to any other donor.

With corporations you have to have a lot of demographic data and psychographic data. You need to tell them essentially who the audience is that will want to see the film. You have to show to them the psychographic data. Here is the age group; here is where they live, and here is how much they spend on these kinds of products.

The corporation is thinking, "I want more good will from people who buy my products. How will your film help me impact those people I want to reach?" You have to make this connection for them.

Where do you think is the best place for filmmakers to go for funding?

Your mother, your father! You know Carole, it is too big of a question to answer generally. It depends on several factors. One factor is what type of piece are you making? Some work is more appropriate for some venues of fund raising than others. If you are making an independent narrative feature film you probably don't want to go to private foundations. On the other hand, if you are making a social issue documentary then you absolutely do want to go to private foundations.

I am recommending that everyone go to individuals as much as they can. It is an underused resource of funding for most filmmakers. It is so proactive and there is a lot of money available but there are some instances where individuals would be impossible, like short experimental work.

You may be stuck paying for it yourself, or there are a handful of foundations that are interested in this type of film, but you won't get money from individuals.

Then you feel at the moment individuals are a good untapped resource?

Oh, yes, absolutely. Especially now because this is a horrible time to go to corporations and foundations because of the economy.

Do you have any advice you would like to give emerging filmmakers and those that have been in the trenches before?

My major advice to every filmmaker is to step back from all of this and really try to understand why you are doing this work at all. This is why my consulting is so very different, and why when I begin a relationship with a filmmaker I make them go through this thing I call an initial consultation. A major part of my consultation with the filmmaker means understanding, clarifying and committing to a mission statement before they go on with the film. What is your mission statement as a filmmaker? Why are you making films? Corollary to this is the question of vision. What do you see yourself doing in the future? The third thing is have you identified your set of values?

Mission, vision, and values. Those three things are at the very heart of my work with everyone I work with.

I say to the beginning, the emerging, the seasoned, the veteran filmmaker, "Have you clarified these things first? Because until you do and unless you do, you will not be as effective at filmmaking as you could be!"

When I tell filmmakers this before we consult, they scratch their heads and wonder what I am talking about. Then I say, "Well, either we can talk about these, and you work with me, or we don't."

This is the way I work. I guarantee if you speak to ninety-nine percent of the people I work with [they] will verify how beneficial this work is.

How many ways do you work with people, and how do they reach you?

The easiest way is to go to my web site at www.warshawski.com. On my page called "Workshops" there is a detailed description of my initial consultation service. That is the fastest way to find out how I work. I am very clear and detailed about what I want from a filmmaker before we talk, and then what they will get during that initial consultation. That is how I begin every relationship with every filmmaker. After that I am very flexible. I work on a retainer by the hour or by the day if the filmmaker and I both agree we are a good match. That is one thing we discover in our initial conversation.

Which area is your ongoing work with filmmakers directed?

The filmmaker always comes to me because they are desperate for money. The reason they have called me is they have hit the wall and are desperate for funds. Then they get the good news and bad news from me. The bad news is I can't help them with the money until they work on these things with me. The good news is if they can get these other things straightened out they will absolutely increase their effectiveness as a fundraising filmmaker. But whether or not we will continue to work together depends on a lot of factors. For one thing, usually the initial consultation gives the filmmaker enough work to keep them busy for a year without me.

On the other hand I have had relationships that went on for years afterward where I kept working on a couple of tracks. One of these is career development. What I can do is help someone keep in context how their current project is just a piece of a larger puzzle. Filmmakers can wear blinders. They can get so involved in their projects they can't see the forest for the trees. I help to keep bringing them back to the larger picture and that way they can make more powerful strategic decisions.

Then another track we work on is fundraising. I don't do the fundraising or write the grants, but I help keep them on course, spot check, and look at proposals. But I am much more interested in the entire life of the filmmaker.

This must be very rewarding work for you Morrie.

Yes, it is. I love the work I do.

Every ceiling, when reached, becomes a floor, upon which one walks as a matter of course and prescriptive right.
—Aldous Huxley

SPONSORSHIP IS DEAD
By Daniel Sherrett

Daniel Sherrett is the CEO of EVENT TV International Entertainment Marketing, a corporation that works with producers and corporate America to bring a variety of television, film, entertainment and cultural projects to fruition via corporate/brand partnerships.

The following was written and edited by Daniel Sherrett:

"SPONSORSHIP IS DEAD" - is how I recently addressed a large group of television and film producers at a conference in New York City.

The obvious reaction from the crowd was a deep breath and an "OH NO!" as so many producers have relied on sponsorship to help fund their projects.

I partially relieved the tension in the room by announcing, "partnerships are alive and well." But, there was still a lot of explaining to do.

When I say, "sponsorship is dead," what I mean is that sponsorship, and the way it has been presented, is yesterday's way of approaching corporations for production and promotional funding.

"Sponsorship" is now perceived by potential corporate partners as, "a lot of money for very little return."

Let's take a look at the definitions of Sponsorship and Partnership:

Sponsorship

One that finances a project or an event carried out by another person or group, especially a business enterprise that pays for radio or television programming in return for ***advertising*** time. (dictionary.com)

Partnership

A relationship between individuals or groups that is characterized by mutual cooperation and responsibility, as for the achievement of a specified goal. (dictionary .com)

A contract between two or more competent persons for joining together their money, goods, labor, and skill, or any or all of them, under an understanding that there shall be a communion of profit between them. (Online plain English dictionary).

Note the major difference

- Sponsorship - return - advertising
- Partnership - return - ROI, (return on investment).

ROI, or return on investment is what the new breed of marketing executives at corporations are looking for.

The old "Sponsorship Model" could offer a sponsor little more than opening and closing program billboards and maybe a commercial spot or two within a program. The sponsor could buy the same media exposure or media value from a television broadcaster for a mere fraction of what the producer needed in funding to bring their project to fruition.

Corporate Partnership Model

As previously stated, corporations are looking for tangible returns on their investments. The old days of, "let's sponsor this because we like it," or "because the CEO is particularly interested in that subject matter," are gone.

The new breed of marketing/communications executive is looking out for the best interests of the company and has been mandated to make sure that getting involved with a television program or film had better be in line with the company's current marketing, sales and communications strategies.

Now that many people who are looking for funding have heard that partnership has replaced sponsorship as the latest buzz-word to get in the door, most are simply approaching potential corporate partners with the same old sponsorship package, masking it as a partnership. That won't fly!

Corporations are looking for true business partnerships. Again let's look at the definition of a partnership: *A contract between two or more competent persons for joining together their money, goods, labor, and skill, or any or all of them, under an understanding that there shall be a communion of profit between them.* AHA.... There's that ugly word *profit. This could just as easily say that there shall be a return on investment.*

In order for those of us who are on the "asking for funding" side to better understand what **return on investment** means to our potential corporate partner(s) we are going to have to do some research and find out how they run their businesses.

Return on investment will mean different things to different companies, based on many varying factors: type of business, products' demographic target, company mission statement and philosophy, business location(s), distribution, etc.

ROI isn't always about selling more goods. In the case of the insurance and financial services industries, corporate partnerships will likely be more about creating good will in the community and seeing longer-term benefits. It will be particularly important to these industries to have cal "grass-roots" involvement, via their branches, agents, etc.

Let's take a look at a typical corporation and the working groups within that corporation that should be affected by the company's decision to enter into a corporate partnership with a film, TV series/special, event, etc.

Corporate Communications

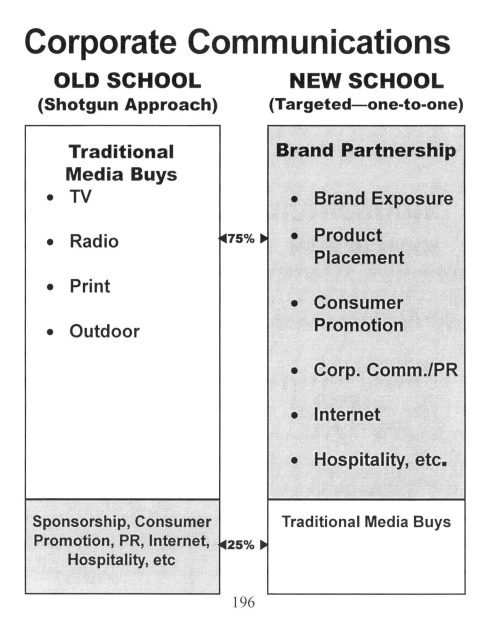

OLD SCHOOL	NEW SCHOOL
(Shotgun Approach)	**(Targeted—one-to-one)**

Traditional Media Buys		Brand Partnership
• TV		• Brand Exposure
• Radio	◄75%►	• Product Placement
• Print		• Consumer Promotion
• Outdoor		• Corp. Comm./PR
		• Internet
		• Hospitality, etc.
Sponsorship, Consumer Promotion, PR, Internet, Hospitality, etc	◄25%►	Traditional Media Buys

XYZ Corp:
- Marketing
- Advertising
- Website - online strategy
- Sales - sales force
- Consumer/Trade Promotion - contests, sampling, etc.
- Corporate Communications/PR
- Retail partners (If products sold at retail).
- Agents (If products or services sold through agents).
- Trade shows
- Hospitality - hosting
- Employee relations - incentives
- Merchandising - books, posters, apparel, etc.
- Donations/Cause Marketing (supporting charities).

Now, when crafting and pitching the corporate partner's benefits package, there are a lot more "hot-buttons" to push and a greater opportunity for the corporate partner to see a return-on-investment. Developing a partnership that gets many areas of the corporation involved creates excitement within the company and a healthy competitiveness between the divisions to get as much out of the partnership as possible.

Money for Corporate Partnerships, (sponsorship as many may still call it) is available, we on the asking side just have to work harder to get it and earn it.

Keeping the corporate partner satisfied is key. **Fulfillment** is the most important aspect of the process. We promised that we were going to do this and that for the money/ funding so we'd better come through. There's no question that this is a lot more work than the old "Sponsorship Model", but, if well executed the new "Partnership Model" will keep corporate clients coming back for the "next big project."

Because the new process is a lot more work, many producers/property rights holders will look to a specialist that is experienced in marrying corporations with media properties and one that has a good track record within the industry. Most producers want to produce and simply do not have the time to research, create, pitch and fulfill a corporate partner relationship.

Now is as good a time as ever to be looking for a corporate partner. As traditional media and its audiences become more fragmented and the cost of media less efficient, many corporations are looking for more creative and tangible ways to reach their customers and potential customers. Some people call it niche marketing, others one-on-one marketing, but whatever you call it there is a trend to move budgets away from traditional mass media advertising. The old "shotgun" approach doesn't work anymore, it's too inefficient, that's why we've seen such a proliferation of specialty TV networks, magazines, websites, etc.

To take this several steps further, a corporation can now partner with targeted media properties, (TV programs, Films) that will deliver the exact audience they're looking for and be able to leverage their partnership investment by integrating many aspects of their business **(see XYZ Corp. above).**

Many producers are nervous that by bringing on a corporate partner they might be giving up some creative freedom around their projects. In most cases, the senior marketing/communications staff at corporations are very "media savvy" and do not want to interfere with the content of a program or film. They're "buying in" because they like the content that was presented.

They also realize that the general public is now more media savvy than ever and they don't want to do anything that might turn the audience off.

In developing the corporate partner's package, creativity is more about what can be done, (leveraged) outside the program/film than within. This can be a big win for the producer, especially if the corporate partner is directed to spend a portion of the partnership funds on promoting the program or the film. This usually results in bigger audiences for the producer and the corporate partner. Everybody wins!

Product placement can be an important element of the partnership. The partner's product should only be placed within the program/film if and when appropriate. Again, most corporations understand this, but if the shot calls for a car to drive by "why can't it be a Ford"?

When pitching potential corporate partners, challenge the point person, (should be a senior marketing or communications exec) to invite as many senior managers as possible from as many departments that may be positively effected by the partnership. Your chances of securing a deal will be greater if two or three of the departments see a benefit to their area.

Let's not forget that we're in "Show-Biz"... that's how the corporate partner is going to view the meeting. This should be the best meeting these people have had in a long time. Because we're in "Show-Biz", the corporate partner presentation meeting should be compelling and entertaining. Without going over-the-top, we should be using the latest in presentation technologies. Both electronic and print copies of the presentation should be left behind.

The presentation needs to be scripted and rehearsed, allowing time for lots of comments and questions. We should also be asking questions. No question is a dumb question. Most executives love to talk about what they do and how they do it. This will give us, on the asking side, more insight into the workings of the corporation and will better enable us to satisfy the needs of our corporate partner.

For more information on the subject, contact:

Daniel W. Sherrett, President & CEO
EVENT TV International - Entertainment Marketing
Toll free: 866-410-7066 e-mail: dan@eventtv.tv

Carole Joyce

Bright Feelings

Dear Filmmakers,

The Art of Funding Your Film was created from questions I have received throughout the years from filmmakers just like you. The purpose of the book is to give you as much information as possible to help you create an effective proposal and pitch, and complete all of those funding applications. The book incorporates many new concepts along with some tried and true techniques for funding your films. I sincerely hope you found this book helpful.

I am currently working on a new book that will feature copies of winning applications and interviews with filmmakers. My intent is to give you a follow-up book that has some example applications for you to review and comments from the filmmakers about their process. Please let me know what you want in this new "Winners" book. Just email me at caroleedean@att.net and, if possible, I will be happy to include it.

The goal of the Roy W. Dean film grants and my personal goal are to see more documentaries created that "are unique and make a contribution to society." I want these books to give you some valuable insights that will make your artistic journey successful and full of joy.

I take my hat off to all of you. I see so many applicants who wear multiple hats-writer, director, producer, etc., and wonder if you realize how creative you really are.

Many people in this world would give anything to have just one of those talents.

It is a pleasure to work with and for such talented people. Keep up the good work. You are changing this world for the better!

May you always walk in beauty,

Carole Dean

Carole Dean
1455 Mandalay Beach Rd
Oxnard, Ca 93035

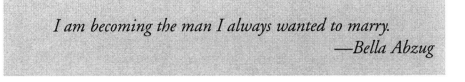

I am becoming the man I always wanted to marry.
—*Bella Abzug*

APPENDIX

DISCLAIMER OF LIABILITY, HTML COMPATIBILITY, OR ENDORSEMENT: WHILE EVERY EFFORT IS MADE TO ENSURE THE TIMELINESS AND ACCURACY OF THE INFORMATION AND DOCUMENTS REFERENCED, CAROLE DEAN PUBLISHING AND FROM THE HEART PRODUCTIONS ASSUMES NO LEGAL LIABILITY OR RESPONSIBILITY FOR THE COMPLETENESS OR USEFULNESS OF ANY INFORMATION DISCLOSED. NOR DO WE ENSURE COMPATIBILITY WITH PAST, CURRENT OR FUTURE VERSIONS OF YOUR FAVORITE BROWSER.

REFERENCES DO NOT CONSTITUTE AN ENDORSEMENT OF THOSE PARTIES OR ANY REPRESENTATION AS TO THE ACCURACY OR OTHERWISE OF THE INFORMATION SUPPLIED BY THEM. CAROLE DEAN PUBLISHING AND FROM THE HEART PRODUCTIONS ASSUMES NO LIABILITY FOR ACTS, ERRORS, OR OMISSIONS BY OFF-SITE PARTIES OR THE MATERIALS SUPPLIED BY THEM.

APPENDIX A: PRODUCTION RESOURCES FOR PUBLIC TELEVISION

American Public Television Producer's Handbook
http://www.aptonline.org/aptonline.nsf/Producers?Openpage

Enhancing Education, a Producer's Guide
http://enhancinged.wgbh.org/
If you are going to get funding for your public television program, you will need to have an educational outreach plan. This site is essentially a producer's guide on how to maximize the educational impact of their projects. The guide will give you a deeper understanding of how public broadcasting approaches educational theory. You can see what other projects have developed as educational enhancements and how they've done it, and discover the basics of educational outreach by exploring various educational formats.

New Voices, New Media Fund
http://www.cpb.org/tv/funding/nvnm/
CPB has allocated up to $2 million this year to create the New Voices, New Media Fund. We see this Fund as one tool in public broadcasting's effort to demonstrate the potential of digital technology to support and enhance our core qualities and core business. The New Voices, New Media Fund is part of the "I, too, am America" Initiative.

Public Broadcasting Service (PBS)
http://www.pbs.org/
1320 Braddock Place
Alexandria, VA 22314-1698
Tel. 703-739-5000
Fax. 703-739-0775

Producing for PBS
http://www.pbs.org/producers/

Independent Television Service (ITVS)
http://www.itvs.org/
501 York Street
San Francisco, CA 94110
Tel. 415-356-8383
Fax: 415-356-8391
E-mail: itvs@itvs.org

Latino Public Broadcasting (LPB)
http://www.lpbp.org/
Marlene Dermer, Executive Director
6777 Hollywood Boulevard, Suite 500
Los Angeles, CA 90028
Ph. 323-466-7110
Fax. 323-466-7521

National Black Programming Consortium
http://nbpc.tv/old_site/ibf/
145 East 125th Street, Suite 220
New York, NY 10035
Tel. 212-828-7588
Fax. 212-828-7930
E-mail: nbpcinfo@blackstarcom.org

National Asian American Telecommunications Association (NAATA)
http://www.naatanet.org/
145 9th St, Suite #350
San Francisco, CA 94103
Tel. 415-863-0814
Fax: 415-863-7428
E-mail: naata@naatanet.org

Native American Public Telecommunications, Inc. (NAPT)
http://www.nativetelecom.org/
P. O. Box 83111
Lincoln, Nebraska 68501
Tel. 402-472-3522
Fax. 402-472-8675
E-mail: fblythe@unlinfo.unl.edu

Pacific Islanders in Communications (PIC)
http://pic.wetserver.net/index.jsp
1221 Kapiolani Blvd
Suite #6A-4
Honolulu, Hawaii 96814
Tel. 808-591-0059
Fax. 808-591-1114
E-mail: info@piccom.org

National Science Foundation (NSF)
http://www.nsf.gov/

4201 Wilson Boulevard
Arlington, VA 22230
Tel. 703-306-1234
Fax. 703-306-0250
E-mail: info@nsf.gov

National Endowment for the Arts (NEA)
http://www.arts.endow.gov/
1100 Pennsylvania Avenue
Washington, D.C. 20506
Tel. 202-682-5400

National Endowment for the Humanities (NEH)
http://www.neh.gov/
1100 Pennsylvania Avenue
Washington, D.C. 20506
Tel. 1-800-NEH-1121
202-606-8400

U.S. Department of Education
http://www.ed.gov/

The Carnegie Corporation of New York
http://www.carnegie.org/

The Ford Foundation
http://www.fordfound.org/

MacArthur Foundation
http://www.macfound.org/

The Pew Charitable Trusts
http://www.pewtrusts.com/

Rockefeller Foundation
http://www.rockfound.org

Understand the PBS Greenlight Process: Getting PBS to Yes, by Jackie Conciatore
http://itvs.org/producers/pbstoyes.html

WNET
www.thirteen.org

APPENDIX B: INTERNET SEARCH TOOLS

About.com (http://about.com)

ListOfLists.com (http://listoflists.com)

Metacrawler (http://www.metacrawler.com)

Northern Light (www.northernlight.com)

ProFusion (http://www.profusion.com)

Search Engine Watch (www.searchenginewatch.com)

Sink or Swim:Internet Search Tools & Techniques (www.ouc.bc.ca/libr/connect96/search.htm)

APPENDIX C: DATABASES, RESOURCES & TOOLS

Free Databases

Action Without Borders
www.idealist.org
Searchable index to more than 21,500 nonprofit and community organizations in more than 150 countries. Search by organization name, location, or mission keyword.

Charles Steward Mott Foundation
http://www.mott.org/news/detail-preview.asp?newsid=187
Detailed fact sheets on every grant made by the foundation since 1995. Updated quarterly.

European Foundation Centre
http://www.efc.be
Established in 1989 by seven of Europe's leading foundations, the EFC today serves a core membership of more than 200 members, associates and subscribers; 250 community philanthropy initiatives; as well as a further 48,000 organizations linked through a network of information and support centers in 37 countries worldwide.

FastWeb
http://www.fastweb.com/.
Searchable database of more than 400,000 private sector scholarships, fellowships, grants, and loans from more than 3,000 sources for all levels of higher education.

Ford Foundation
http://www.fordfound.org/grants_db/view_grant_by_keyword.cfm
www.fordfound.org
Includes three years of grants made by the foundation. Updated quarterly. Search by program or keyword. A good place to check out who got funded!

Foundation Finder (Foundation Center)
http://lnp.fdncenter.org/finder.html
Search by name for basic information about foundations. More than 70,000 private and community foundations in the U.S.

Foundations On-Line
www.foundations.org/index.html
Browse the foundation directory, pick a listed foundation, search any foundation's information page or search any foundation's home page. Foundation home pages may

contain downloadable information such as grant applications, periodical and financial reports, and e-mail capabilities.

GrantSmart

www.grantsmart.org

Find private foundations with areas of support that match your needs. You can also determine if an organization specifically excludes proposals in a particular area. This can save you time and effort when applying for grants.

Kellogg Foundation Online Database of Current Grants

http://www.wkkf.org

To access database select "grants" then "search database." Includes all of Kellogg's grants since 1991.

Pew Charitable Trusts Grants Database

http://www.pewtrusts.com

Includes every grant awarded since 1995.

GuideStar

http://www.guidestar.org/

The GuideStar Web site is produced by Philanthropic Research, Inc., a 501(c)(3) public charity founded in 1994. GuideStar's mission is to revolutionize philanthropy and nonprofit practice with information. Search grantmakers websites by keyword. Also view grantmakers tax return forms.

Fee-Based Databases

Foundation Grants for Individuals on CD-ROM

Located at most major city libraries for free! Offers high-speed searching of foundations and public charities that provide support for individuals. 4,200 foundations and public charities that support education, research, arts, general welfare, and more. Search fields include: fields of interest, types of support, geographic focus, company name, school name, grantmaker name, grantmaker city, grantmaker state, and text search.

GrantSelect

http://www.grantselect.com/

GrantSelect is the online version of the GRANTS Database, produced by The Oryx Press, containing over 10,000 funding opportunities provided by over 3,400 sponsoring organizations. Michigan State university faculty, staff, and students can identify additional funding opportunities related to film by searching this database. You can fill out the form for a free, no obligation 7-day trial.

GrantsWeb

www.srainternational.org/newweb/grantsweb/index.cfm

Resources & Tools

Chamber of Commerce
www.chamber.com/

DMA Nonprofit Federation
www.the-dma.org/nonprofitfederation/index.html

Directory of financial aids for women, 2001-2003 http://www.netLibrary.com/
urlapi.asp?action=summary&v=1&bookid=67836
NetLibrary, 2002. Available via World Wide Web.
Access may be limited to NetLibrary affiliated libraries (check with your local library).

Edgar Database (U.S. Securities & Exchanged Commission)
http://www.sec.gov/edgar/searchedgar/webusers.htm

Fund-Raising and Foundation Research
www.usc.edu/dept/source/found.htm

Fund-Raising Forum
www.raise-funds.com/forum.html

Fund-Raising.com
www.fund-raising.com/

Fundsnet Services Online
www.fundsnetservices.com/

Nonprofit Guides
http://npguides.org
Database of grantwriting tools for nonprofits

Idealist.org
www.idealist.org/

Internet Movie Database
http://us.imdb.com/

Internet Nonprofit Center
http://nonprofits.org/

Internet Prospector
www.internet-prospector.org/

National Alliance for Media Arts and Culture
www.namac.org

National Endowment for the Arts
www.arts.endow.gov

Nonprofit Gateway
http://firstgov.gov/Topics/Nonprofit.shtml

Online Fundraising Resources Center
www.fund-online.com/

Philanthropy News Digest (PND)
www.fdncenter.org/pnd/index.jhtml

The Grantsmanship Center
www.tgci.com/

Virtual Foundation
www.virtualfoundation.org/

GrantsNet
www.grantsnet.org/

Grantmakers in the Arts
www.giarts.org/

APPENDIX D: ONLINE ARTICLES

Contract Law as a Remedy for Story Theft
Excerpt from Contracts for the Film & Television Industry (2nd Edition), by Mark Litwak http://www.marklitwak.com/cl_remedy.html

Copyright Registration of Scripts & Films, by Mark Litwak
http://www.marklitwak.com/litwak.dir/FORM%20PA%20final.htm

Filmmaker's Bill of Rights, by Mark Litwak
http://www.marklitwak.com/bill.htm

Grantwriting 101: Tips for Novice Proposal Writers, by Julie Seewald Bornhoeft, CFRE
http://charitychannel.com/article_116.shtml

How to Throw a Fundraising Houseparty
an audio segment by Morrie Warshawski which first appeared on NPR's Marketplace Radio. Download available at: http://www.warshawski.com/books.html

Love. War and the Joy of Seeking Production Financing, by Patric Hedlund
http://www.forests.com

Movie Merchandising, by Mark Litwak
http://www.marklitwak.com/movmerc.html

Obtaining Music For A Motion Picture Soundtrack, by Mark Litwak
http://www.marklitwak.com/music_mpsound.htm

The Program Description — Giving Your Ideas Life, by Julie Seewald Bornhoeft, CFRE
http://charitychannel.com/article_3051.shtml

Protecting Film Investors, by Mark Litwak
http://www.marklitwak.com/investor.html

Show Me the Money, an interview with Morrie Warshawski
http://newenglandfilm.com/news/archives/02december/money.htm

Tips for Winning Federal Grants, by Lawrence H. Trachtman
http://charitychannel.com/article_120.shtml

APPENDIX E: PRINT RESOURCES

A Bread Crumb Trail Through the PBS Jungle: The Producer's Survival Guide,
by Patric Hedlund
ISBN 1-57844-C48-3. Available at http://www.forests.com/breadcrumb

Contracts for the Film and Television Industry, by Mark Litwak

Corporate Foundation Profiles, Published by The Foundation Center, NY

Corporate Giving Yellowpages, Published by Taft Group, Rockville, MD

Dealmaking in the Film and Television Industry: From Negotiations Through Final Contracts,
by Mark Litwak

The Directory of Corporate and Foundation Givers, Published by Taft Group, Rockville, MD

Directory of Grants in the Humanities, Oryx Press, Westport, Ct.

Directory of International Corporate Giving in America and Abroad, Published by Taft Group,
Rockville, MD

Filmmakers & Financing: Business Plans For Independents, by Louise Levison, Focal Press

Foundation Grants to Individuals, Published by the Foundation Center, NY

The Four Agreements: A Practical Guide to Personal Freedom, by Don Miguel Ruiz

*The Fundraising Houseparty: How to Get Charitable Donations From Individuals in a Houseparty
Setting,*
by Morrie Warshawski

Grant Finder: Arts & Humanities, St. Martin's Press, inc. NY. 2000

Guide to Private Fortunes, Published by Taft Group, Rockville, MD

Guide to U.S. Foundations, Their Trustees, Officers, and Donors. Published by the Foundation
Center, NY

National Directory of Corporate Giving, Published by The Foundation Center, NY

The Next Step: Distributing Independent Films and Videos, Edited by Morrie Warshawski.

The Producer's Business Handbook (Book & CD-ROM), by John J. Lee, Published by Focal
Press

The Creative Collaboration Between Directors, Writers, and Actors, by Mark Travis
published by Michael Wiese

*Reel Power: The Struggle for Influence and Success in the New Hollywood
Litwak's Multimedia Producer's Handbook,* by Mark Litwak

Shaking the Money Tree: How to Get Grants and Donations for Film and Television - 2nd Edition
by Morrie Warshawski. Michael Wiese Books/LA

Excuse me, Your Life is Waiting: The Astonishing Power of Feelings, by Lynn Grabhorn

APPENDIX F: WRITING RESOURCES

The Elements of Style by William Strunk, Jr.
http://www.bartleby.com/141/

Purdue University's Online Writing Lab
http://owl.english.purdue.edu/

The Writer's Handbook: A Guide to the Essentials of Good Writing
By John B. Karls and Ronald Szymanski

The Writer's Journey: Mythic Structure for Writers
By Christopher Vogler

Writing a Better ITVS Treatment
http://itvs.org/producers/treatment.html

Grant/Proposal Writers

Candace Kavanagh
candacek@sbcglobal.net
323- 913-9800

JanEva Hornbaker
Grant & Proposal Writing, Script Revision, Film Treatments, Editing
eva@SNAFUfilms.com
602-274-1666

APPENDIX G: BUSINESS PROMOTION/ PUBLIC RELATIONS

Cinda Jackson, Director, Choreographer, Teacher
Artistic director *les enfants Magiques*!
323 933 6944

Branwen Edwards
BranwenEdwards@aol.com
Life coach for Carole Dean, whose mission is to have people expand beyond their wildest dreams.

Morrie Warshawski, Arts Consultant/Writer
www.warshawski.com
734-332-9768

Spiritual PR
Tory Jay Berger
friends@netzero.net

APPENDIX H: ORGANIZATIONS

American Film Institute
http://www.afi.com/

American Film Marketing Association
http://www.afma.com/

Archive of American Television (From the Academy of Television Arts & Sciences)
http://www.emmys.org/foundation/archive/index.htm

Business Committee for the Arts, Inc. (BCA)
http://www.bcainc.org/

Center for Entertainment Data
http://www.ceidr.org/

DirectorsNet
http://www.directorsnet.com/index.html

Documentary Educational Resources
http://www.der.org/

Documentary Films.Net
http://documentaryfilms.net/

Filmmakers Alliance
http://www.filmmakersalliance.com/

HollywoodU.com, Dov S-S Simens, Founder
http://hollywoodu.com; info@webfilmschool.com
1223 Olympic Blvd, Santa Monica, CA 90404
1-800-366-3456, 1-310-399-6699

Independent Feature Project
http://www.ifp.org

International Documentary Association
www.documentary.org

MIPCOM World TV market
http://www.mipcom.com
World TV market

Motion Picture Association of America
http://www.mpaa.org/

National Association of Theatre Owners
http://www.natoonline.org/

New England Film Archives
http://www.newenglandfilm.com/
Online magazine & resource for 38,000+ local filmmakers & video makers.

SAG
http://www.sag.com

Write News
http://www.writenews.com/

APPENDIX I: FUNDERS

911 MEDIA ARTS CENTER
http://www.911media.org
Offers access to media making tools for artists at a low cost

A. J. MUSTE INSTITUTE339
Lafayette StreetNew York, NY 10012
Phone: 212-533-4335
Fax: 212-228-6193
Email: ajmusteinst@igc.org
Website: www.ajmuste.org
Funds projects that promote social change.

ACADEMY OF MOTION PICTURE ARTS & SCIENCES
8949 Wilshire Boulevard
Beverly Hills CA 90211-1972
Phone: 310-247-3059
Fax: 310-859-9351
Richard Miller Phone: 310-247-3000
ampas@oscars.org http://www.oscars.org
Send legal-size SASE after January 1 to receive entry form $2,000, $1,500 and
$1,000 awards in dramatic, experimental, documentary, animation.

AGAPE FOUNDATION FUND FOR NONVIOLENT SOCIAL CHANGE
1095 Market St., Suite 304
San Francisco, CA 94103
Phone: (415) 701-8707
Fax: 701-8706
www.agapefn.org; info@agapefn.org

Western states only. Funds films/videos that promote the use of nonviolence. Supports films/video that are unable to secure funding from traditional sources.

AKONADI FOUNDATION
488 Ninth Street
Oakland, CA 94607
http://www.akonadi.org/index.htmlinfo@akonadi.org
Supports a variety of programmatic approaches including research, policy work, advocacy, litigation, organizing, media, arts, diversity training, education and other tools in their anti-racism work.

AMERICAN ANTIQUARIAN SOCIETY (AAS)
Contact: Artists and Writers Fellowships
American Antiquarian Society
185 Salisbury St.
Worcester, MA 01609-1634
Phone: 508.471.2131 or 471.2139 Fax::508.754.9069
e-mail: jmoran@mwa.org
www.americanantiquarian.org/artistfellowship.
Calling for applications for visiting fellowships for historical research by creative and performing artists, writers, filmmakers, journalists and other persons whose goals are to produce imaginative, non-formulaic works dealing with pre-twentieth-century American history.

AMERICAN FILM INSTITUTE
P.O. Box 27999
2021 N. Western Avenue
Los Angeles CA 90027
Phone: 213-856-7691
Fax: 213-476-4578
http://www.afionline.com
Call, write or check website for application instructions. 3 week training program for mid-career women in the media arts to learn about narrative directing and to apply for production grant positions.

AMERICAN PUBLIC TELEVISION (APT)
120 Boylston Street
Boston, MA 02116
http://www.aptonline.org

Phone:(617) 338-4455
Acquires finished programs and develops/produces original programming concepts. Undertakes the distribution of programming that is tailored to specific interests or demographics.

ANNIE E. CASEY FOUNDATION
Attention: Office of the President
701 St. Paul Street
Baltimore, MD 21202
http://www.aecf.org/about/grantguidelines.htm
Fosters public policies, human service reforms, and community supports that more effectively meet the needs of today's vulnerable children and families.

ARTHUR VINING DAVIS FOUNDATIONS
Dr. Jonathan T. Howe, Executive Director
Arthur Vining Davis Foundations
111 Riverside Ave., Ste. 130
Jacksonville, FL 32202-4921
Phone: 904.359.0670
e-mail: arthurvining@msn.com
web: www.jvm.com/davis.
Provides partial support for major educational series assured of airing nationally by PBS. The Foundations prefer proposals for "capstone" grants which assure completion of production funding

ARTISTS' TELEVISION ACCESS
992 Valencia St.
an Francisco CA 94110
http://www.atasite.org ata@atasite.org
Phone: 415-824-3890
Fax: 415-824-0526
Equipment access available at subsidized rates to artists, community organizations, and people on limited incomes.

ASSOCIATION OF INDEPENDENT VIDEO AND FILMMAKERS
304 Hudson Street, 6th floor
New York, NY 10013
Phone: 212-807-1400
Fax: 212-463-8519
Email: info@aivf.org

Website: http://aivf.org
Membership organization whose magazine, The Independent, regularly profiles funders of film and video and is considered required reading in the film/video community.

ASTRAEA FOUNDATION
116 East 16th Street, 7th Floor
New York, NY 10003
Phone: 212-529-8021
Fax: 212-982-3321
Email: info@astraea.org
Supports cultural/Media Film/Video on issues involving lesbian, gay, bisexual, and transgender issues

BARBARA DEMING MEMORIAL FUND
P.O. Box 40-1043
Brooklyn, NY 11240-1043
Offers up to $1,000 per grant, open to women whose projects speak for peace and social justice

BAY AREA VIDEO COALITION
2727 Mariposa Street, 2nd Floor
San Francisco, CA 94110
Phone: 415-861-4328
Fax: 415-861-4316
Email: awards@bavc.org
Website: www.bavc.org/resources/grants
San Francisco Bay Area only, with the exception of the Phelan Award, which is available to artists born in California, regardless of current residence.

Bogliasco Foundation
http://www.liguriastudycenter.org/
Accepting applications for Fellowships during the 2003-2004 academic year. Deadlines: January 15, 2003, for residencies during the fall-winter semester beginning in September 2003, and April 15, 2003, for the winter-spring semester beginning in February 2004. Grants semester-long fellowships for scholars or artists to work at the Liguria Study Center in Bogliasco, Italy, near Genoa. The Fellowship is designed for advanced creative work or scholarly research in

archaeology, architecture, classics, dance, film or video, history, landscape architecture, literature, music, philosophy, theater, or visual arts.

BOSTON FILM/VIDEO FOUNDATION
1126 Boylston St. #201
Boston, MA 02215
Phone: 617-536-1540
Email: info@bfvf.orgWebsite: www.bfvf.org
Various funding for New England film/video makers

CALIFORNIA ARTS COUNCIL
1300 I Street, Suite 930
Sacramento, CA 95814
Phone: 916-322-6555
Fax: 916-322-6575
Offers grants & programs for film & media makers

CALIFORNIA DOCUMENTARY PROJECT
Los Angeles office: 213.623.5993; San Francisco office: 415.391.1474; San Diego office: 619.232.4020; e-mail: info@calhum.org; web: www.calhum.org.
Designed to encourage documentarians of the new millennium to create enduring images and text of contemporary California.

CARNEGIE ENDOWMENT FOR INTERNATIONAL PEACE
Website: http://www.ceip.orge-mail: info@ceip.org
Private, nonprofit organization dedicated to advancing cooperation between nations and promoting active international engagement by the United States. Founded in 1910, its work is nonpartisan and dedicated to achieving practical results.

CAROLE FIELDING STUDENT PRODUCTION & RESEARCH GRANTS
http://www.ufva.org/fieldingmain.html
Competitive awards presented annually to students whose research and production projects meet rigorous standards of academic scholarship. Up to $4,000 is available for film, video, or multimedia production and up to $1,000 is available for research projects in historical, critical, theoretical or experimental studies of film or video.

CATCHLIGHT FILMS
www.catchlightfilms.com/directory.html

Invests in eligible films through all unfinished stages of post-production: editing, music scoring or clearance, post-supervision, deliverables, negative cut, lab fees, etc.

CENTER FOR ALTERNATIVE MEDIA AND CULTURE
P.O. Box 0832
Radio City Station, New York, NY 10101
Phone: 212.977.2096
Email: tvnatfans@aol.com.
Supports independent media projects in post-production that address the economy, class issues, poverty, women, war and peace, race, and labor.

CENTER FOR INDEPENDENT DOCUMENTARY
1608 Beacon St.
Waban, MA 01268
Phone: 508.528.7279
Email:info@documentaries.org
Web: www.documentaries.org.
Multiple Grant Programs. Also provides services on a sliding scale and may select one or two projects a year to receive services for free. Seeking proposals on an ongoing basis from independent producers for the production of documentaries on contemporary issues.

CHANGE, INC.
Box 54 Tapiva, FL 33924
Phone: 212-473-3742
Fax: 212-995-8022
Emergency grants for artists in all disciplines needing help with rent, medical expenses, utility bills, fire damage, etc. Grants up to $1000.

CHARLES AND LUCILLE KING FAMILY FOUNDATION
http://www.kingfoundation.org/
Provides scholarships to outstanding undergraduate students in television and film production. Post Production Grants for outstanding MFA projects at the University of California, Los Angeles and the University of Southern California.

CHIAPAS MEDIA PROJECT (CMP)
http://www.chiapasmediaproject.org

A bi-national partnership that provides video equipment, computers and training, enabling marginalized indigenous and campesino communities in Southern Mexico the opportunity to create their own media.

CHICAGO RESOURCE CENTER
104 S. Michigan Ave., Ste. 1220
Chicago, IL 60603
Phone: 312.759.8700
Awards grants to nonprofits that serve the gay/lesbian community

CHICAGO UNDERGROUND FILM FUND
3109 North Western Ave.
Chicago, IL 60618
Phone: 773-327-FILM
Fax: 773-327-3464
Email: info@cuff.org
Web: http://www.cuff.org
Promotes works that pushes the boundaries, defies commercial expectations and transcends the mainstream of independent filmmaking.

COLUMBIA FOUNDATION
One Lombard Street, Suite 305
San Francisco, CA 94111
Phone: 415-986-5179
Email: carolyn@columbia.org
Web: http://www.columbia.org/index.htm
The foundation gives priority to Bay Area film makers; to films or videos that will be used by Columbia Foundation-funded public-interest organizations to further their work in human rights and sustainable communities and economies; and to projects for which a grant of $5,000 to $25,000 makes a difference in getting the project started or completed.

COMPTON FOUNDATION
http://www.comptonfoundation.org
There are no cut-off dates for discretionary grants. Focuses most of its grant-making in the areas of Peace & World Order, Population, and the Environment. Most of the Foundation's grants for Culture & the Arts are discretionary grants ranging in size from $200 to $10,000.

CORPORATION FOR PUBLIC BROADCASTING
901 E St. NW
Washington, DC 20004-2037
Phone: 202.879.9734
Fax: 202.783.1019
Email: askus@cpb.org
Web: www.cpb.org.
Accepting proposals for the Public Television Future Fund. Open to any project that addresses large-scale opportunities to increase non-federal revenues, create new operating efficiencies and improve the quality of service that stations provide to their communities.

CREATIVE CAPITOL
65 Bleeker St 7th floor
New York NY 10012
Phone: 212-598-9900 Fax:212-598-4934
Email: info@creative-capital.org
Web: www.creative-capital.org
Provides grants to individual artists for specific projects, with an emphasis on experimental work. Disciplines rotate, meaning that media grants are given every other year.

DANCE FILM ASSOCIATION, INC
48 West 21st Street, #907
New York, NY 10010
Phone/Fax: 212-727-0764
Website: http://www.dancefilmsassn.org
Postproduction grant up to $2,000 for films about dance.

DELAWARE HUMANITIES FORUM
100 West 10th St., Ste. 1009
Wilmington, DE 19801
Phone: 302.657.0650
Fax: 302.657.0655
Email: dhfdirector@dhf.org
Web: www.dhf.org/grants.htm.
Supports humanities programs for the public sponsored by nonprofit organizations. Projects should foster an understanding of the humanities disciplines or apply the humanities to topics of public concern.

DIGITAL MEDIA EDUCATION CENTER
Kate Wolf, Digital Media Education Ctr.
5201 SW Westgate Dr., Ste. 114
Portland, OR 97221
Phone: 503.297.2324
Email: kate@filmcamp.com
Web: www.filmcamp.com.
Avid Film Camp program for independent feature directors who are looking for a means to complete their films. Offers Avid-authorized training to career editors.

THE DURFEE FOUNDATION
1453 Third St., Ste. 312
Santa Monica, CA 90401
Phone: 310.899.5120
Fax: 310.899.5121
e-mail: admin@durfee.org
web: www.durfee.org/contact/index.html
Deadline: November 5. Provides ARC (Artists' Resource for Completion) grants which provide rapid, short-term assistance to individual artists in Los Angeles County who wish to complete work for a specific, imminent opportunity that may significantly benefit their careers.

EMPOWERMENT PROJECT
PO Box 2155
Chapel Hill, NC 27515
Phone:919.928.0382
Email: project1@mindspring.com
Web: http://www.empowermentproject.org/
Provides facilities, training and other support for independent producers, artists, activists and organizations working in video and other electronic media.

EXPERIMENTAL TELEVISION CENTER
109 Lower Fairfield Road
Newark Valley, NY 13811
Phone: 607-687-4341
Email: etc@servtech.com
Web: http://www.experimentaltvcenter.org/

Finishing funds (up to $1,500) awarded to individual artists. Presentation funds (up to $1,000) to organizations. Media Arts Technical Assistance Funds (Up to $2,000) to organizations.

FILM ARTS FOUNDATION
info@filmarts.org
Comprehensive training, equipment, information, consultations, and exhibition opportunities to independent filmmakers. Offers multiple programs and grants

FILM/VIDEO ARTS   Film
462 Broadway, Suite #520
New York, NY 10013
Phone: 212.941.8787
Fax: 212.219.8924
Email: info@fva.com
Web: http://www.fva.com/aboutfva/funders_main.htm
Offers programs that encourage interaction between producers of narrative features, documentaries, nontraditional work, shorts, industrials, cable programs, music videos or student projects, by offering them affordable services essential to the creation of their work and the development of their careers.

FILMMAKERS FOUNDATION
5858 Wilshire Blvd.Suite 205
Los Angeles, CA 90036
Phone: (213) 937-5505
FAX: (213) 937-7772
Web: http://members.aol.com/newfilmkrs/
Offers low- or no-cost, high-level programs to give industry professionals the skills and experience to move their careers forward quickly, yet with the confidence that they are building on a solid foundation of knowledge and experience.

FORD FOUNDATION
Director, Media Arts and Culture
320 E. 43rd St., New York, NY 10017
Web: www.fordfound.org/grant/guidelines.html.

Supports public broadcasting and the independent production of film, video and radio programming; and supports efforts to engage diverse groups in work related to the media and to analyze the media's effect on society.

FOUNDATION FOR HELLENIC CULTURE
7 West 57th Street
New York, NY 10019-3402
Phone: (212) 308-6908
Fax: (212) 308-0919
Web: http://www.foundationhellenicculture.com/
The Foundation sponsors art and visual art exhibitions, film screenings, concerts, lectures, theatrical productions, readings, and educational programs.

FOUNDATION FOR MIDDLE EAST PEACE (FMEP)
1761 N St. NW
Washington, DC 20036
Phone: 202-835-3650
Fax: 202-835-3651
Email: President: pcwilcox@fmep.org Editor/Analyst: jeff@fmep.org
Web: http://www.fmep.org/
Committed to "informing Americans on the Israeli-Palestinian conflict and assisting in a peaceful solution that brings security for both peoples." The grantmaking program provides support for organizations and individuals working toward a solution of the Israeli-Palestinian conflict.

FRAMELINE
http://www.frameline.org/
Supports lesbian, gay, bisexual, transgender, visibility through media arts.

FUND FOR JEWISH DOCUMENTARY FILMMAKING
(212) 629-0500 ext. 215
Email at Grants@JewishCulture.org
National Foundation for Jewish Culture can be reached at (212) 629-0500; Fax: (212) 629-0508; E-mail nfjc@jewishculture.org
Established by Steven Spielberg. Fund is designed to support the creation of original documentary films and videos that promote thoughtful consideration of Jewish history, culture, identity, and contemporary issues among diverse public audiences.

FUND FOR WOMEN ARTISTS
www.womenarts.org
The Fund for Women Artists is a non-profit arts service organization dedicated to increasing the diversity and employment of women in the arts

GLASER FOUNDATION
P.O. Box 91123
Seattle, WA 98111
Email: grants@glaserfoundation.org
Focuses on three program areas: progress definition and measurement; animal advocacy; and socially conscious media. In each of these areas, the Foundation develops and pursues its own initiatives and also provides funding support to other nonprofit organizations.

HARBURG FOUNDATION
225 Lafayette Street Room 813
New York, NY 10012
Phone: 212.343.9453
Email:yipharburg@choreographics.com
Advances and promotes new works of American political art, especially those efforts which speak to cultural and societal issues. Television, videos, shows, concerts, radio programs, and all artistic media.

HARVESTWORKS
Web: http://www.harvestworks.org
Contact Director Carol Parkinson for more information @ 212.431.1130
Various deadlines. New Works Residencies 2003, deadline Friday, November 1, 2002. Offers a Digital Media Arts Center to cultivate artistic talent using electronic technologies. Also offers various programs, production studios, grant opportunities, education, communal lab practice and distribution.

HAYMARKET PEOPLE'S FUND
42 Seaverns Avenue
Boston, MA 02130
Phone: 617-522-7676
Fax: 617-522-9580
Email: haymarket@igc.org
Web: http://www.haymarket.org/index.html
Support for New England film/video makers for films with strong connection to community organizing work.

HBO AMERICA UNDERCOVER
Send proposal or tape to
Greg Rhem, HBO, 1100 Sixth Ave., NY, NY 10036
Phone: 212.512.1670
Fax: 212.512.8051
Provides production funds for American indie docs; CINEMAX REEL LIFE acquires completed docs or offers finishing funds for partially completed projects.

HERMES FOUNDATION
13600 Shaker Blvd. #802
Cleveland, OH 44120
Phone: 216-751-1100
Email: senex@msn.com
Especially interested in gay/lesbian issues. Grants up to $1,000

HOLLYWOOD FILM FOUNDATION
433 N. Camden Dr., Ste. 600
Beverly Hills, CA 90210
Web: www.hff.org/grants/application.html
Experimental, Digital Moviemaking, Post-Production, and Partial Budget Grants for up to 50% of budget. Projects must have a first or second time feature director and/or producer and must be budgeted under $5 million; 75% of the production must take place in the State of California.

IFP/CHICAGO PRODUCTION FUND
Phone: 312.435.1825
Fax: 312.435.1828
Email: infoifpmw@aol.com
Web: www.ifp.org.
Win an in-kind donation of production equipment and services, valued at up to $85,000 for your next short film. Applicants must be IFP/Chicago members, and the film must be shot in the Midwest region.

IFP/LOS ANGELES PROJECT
Mentoring and training program that provides young people with exposure, experience, and connections in the film industry. The program supports filmmakers

from traditionally under-represented communities through mentorships, workshops, and screenings.

ILLINOIS HUMANITIES COUNCIL MEDIA GRANTS
203 N. Wabash Ave., Ste. 2020
Chicago, IL 60601-2417
Phone: 312.422.5580
Email: ihc@prairie.org
Web: www.prairie.org
Funding for development (up to $4,000) or production (up to $10,000). Projects must relate centrally and unambiguously to the humanities, have clear potential for reaching a large public audience and be made by producers whose work demonstrates imagination and technical skill.

INDEPENDENT TELEVISION SERVICE (ITVS)
51 Federal St., 1st Floor
San Francisco, CA 94107
Phone: 415.356.8383
Fax: 415.356.8391
Email: marlene_velasco@ itvs.org
Web: www.itvs.org
Various programs and support for video and filmmakers

INSTITUTE OF NOETIC SCIENCES
475 Gate Fire Road, Suite 300
Sausalito, CA 94965
Phone: 415-331-5650 Fax: (415) 331-5673
Email: ions@well.com.
Deadline for applications is usually March 1. Offers an annual Hartley Film Award of $10,000 for production of a film or video which addresses subjects of relevance to the Institute's mission, including consciousness research, mind-body health, meditation, creative altruism, and other areas.

JANE MORRISON MEMORIAL FILM FUND
PO Box 7380
Portland, ME 04112
Phone: 207- 761-2440
Web: http://www.mainecf.org

The annual submission deadliwone is May 15. Offers a fellowship and various support including educational opportunities for filmmakers who are in the early stages of career development. Preference given but not restricted to those residing in Maine.

JEROME FOUNDATION
125 Park Square Ct., 400 Sibley St.
St. Paul, MN 55101-1928
Phone: 651.224.9431
Fax: 651.224.3439
Grant program for individual media artists living and working in New York City. Serves primarily film and video artists.

JOHN D. AND CATHERINE T. MACARTHUR FOUNDATION
Letters of inquiry only (2-3 pages). Requests for proposals by invitation. The John D. and Catherine T. MacArthur Foundation
140 S. Dearborn St.
Chicago, IL 60603
Phone: 312.726.8000
Email: 4answers@macfdn.org
Web: www.macfdn.org.
Key executives: Alyce Myatt, program Officer for Media; Woodward Wickham, Vice President, Public Affairs and the General Program.
Partial support for selected documentary series and independent films intended for national and international broadcast; community outreach related to media; community-based media centers; and public radio. Projects are selected from those that focus on issues that fall within one of the Foundation's two major programs: Human and Community Development or Global Security and Sustainability.

JOHN M. OLIN FOUNDATION
330 Madison Avenue, 22nd floor
New York, New York 10017
phone: (212) 661-2670
fax: (212) 661-5917
http://www.jmof.org/index.htm
Provides support for projects that "reflect or are intended to strengthen the economic, political and cultural institutions upon which the American heritage of constitutional government and private enterprise is based." Provides grants in the areas of American institutions, law and the legal system, public policy research,

and strategic and international studies through support of various programs including on occasion, television and radio programs.

JOHN SIMON GUGGENHEIM FOUNDATION
90 Park Avenue
New York, NY 10016
Phone: (212) 687-4470
FAX (212) 697-3248
Web: http://www.gf.org.
Application deadline is October 1 for U.S. and Canadian citizens' fellowship, December 1 for Latin American and Caribbean citizens' fellowship.
Fellowship competitions: one open to citizens and permanent residents of the United States and Canada, and the other open to citizens and permanent residents of Latin America and the Caribbean. Film and video makers are eligible to apply. The average grant is $28,000

KENTUCKY FOUNDATION FOR WOMEN, INC.
1215 Heyburn Bldg.
332 W. Broadway
Louisville, KY 40202
Phone: 502-562-0045
Fax: 502-561-0420
Email: kfw@kfw.org http://www.kfw.org/
Grants to Kentucky feminist film/video artists.

KQED TV
Scott Dwyer KQED TV
2601 Mariposa Street
San Francisco, CA 94110-1426
inview@kqed.org
Phone: (415) 553-2147.
Interested in presenting challenging independent dramas and documentaries to the Bay Area. Works that are truly independent, unique and fulfill a personal vision. Encourages Independent Producers to approach the station with their projects in development.

LATINO PUBLIC BROADCASTING
Marlene Dermer, Executive Director, Latino Public Broadcasting
6777 Hollywood Blvd., Ste. 500
Los Angeles, CA 90028

Phone: 323.466.7110
Open call for proposals for programs to air on public television. The projects should center around themes and issues that are relevant to Latinos. LPB's mission is to provide a voice for the Latino community throughout the United States with an equitable and accessible funding and distribution mechanism.

LEF FOUNDATION
Web: http://www.lef-foundation.org
Funds are given for projects, programs, and services that encourage "a positive interchange between the arts and the natural urban environment", and may involve visual, media, performing and literary art.

LUCIUS & EVA EASTMAN FUND
P.O. Box 470
Westwood, MA 02090
Phone: 781-329-2473
Contact: Lucius R. Eastman, Pres.
5926 Fiddletown Pl.
San Jose, CA 95120
(phone) 408-268-2083
Supports film/video on social issues.

LYN BLUMENTHAL MEMORIAL FUND FOR INDEPENDENT VIDEO
P.O. Box 3514 Church St. Station
New York, NY 10007
Awards grants for criticism and production.
MARYLAND HUMANITIES COUNCIL
Executive Plaza One, Ste. 503
11350 McCormick Rd.
Hunt Valley, MD 21031-1002
Phone: 410.771.0650
Fax 410.771.0655
Email: pweber@mdhc.org
Web: www.mdhc.org.
Any nonprofit organization may apply for a grant. The council does not fund individuals or for-profit organizations. The project must be a public program, the disciplines of the humanities must be central to the project, humanities scholars must be involved in the project, and funding must support projects that would not normally occur without council support.

MASSACHUSETTS FOUNDATION FOR THE HUMANITIES

Email ekrothman@mfh.org with a brief summary of your proposed project.
Media proposals are accepted only at the November and May deadlines.
Makes grants to support radio programs, films, and videos that explore humanities themes. In FY 2003, media grants are available for pre-production and distribution only.

MASSACHUSETTS FOUNDATION FOR THE HUMANITIES

66 Bridge St.
Northampton, MA 01060
Phone: 413.584.8440
Fax: 413.584.8454
Web: www.mfh.org
Deadline: October 1. Makes major grants each year to support radio programs, films and videos that explore humanities themes. Media grants are available in three categories: pre-production, production and distribution. In amounts over $5,000 and up to $15,000.

MEDIA ALLIANCE

Media Alliance,
c/o WNET
356 W. 58th St.
New York, NY 10019
Phone: 212.560.2919
Assists NYC artists and nonprofit organizations in using state-of-the-art equipment and post-production facilities at reduced rates.

MEDIARIGHTS

104 W. 14th St., 4th Floor
New York, NY 10011
Phone: 646-230-6288
Fax: 646-230-6328
Email: info@mediarights.org
Web: www.mediarights.org
A community website that helps media makers, educators, nonprofits, and activists use documentaries to encourage action and inspire dialogue on contemporary social issues.

MINNESOTA HUMANITIES COMMISSION

Humanities Education Center
987 East Ivy Ave.
Saint Paul, MN 55106

Phone: 651.774.0105
Fax: 651.774.0205
Email: mnhum@thinkmhc.org
Web: www.thinkmhc.org.
Grant applications are reviewed on a rolling basis, so applicants who submit proposals early in the year enhance their likelihood for funding   Provides Media Grants to support humanities projects in radio, film, video and multimedia

MOVING IMAGE FUND
P.O. Box 382866
Cambridge, MA 02238-2866
Phone: 617-492-5333
Email: kathryn@lef-foundation.org
Web: www.lef-foundation.org
Support for New England filmmakers.

NATIONAL ALLIANCE FOR MEDIA ARTS AND CULTURE (NAMAC)
A nonprofit association composed of diverse member organizations who are dedicated to encouraging film, video, audio and online/multimedia arts, and to promoting the cultural contributions of individual media artists.

NATIONAL ASIAN AMERICAN TELECOMMUNICATIONS ASSOCIATION (NAATA)
145 9th St, Suite 350
San Francisco, CA 94103
Web: http://www.naatanet.org/index.html
Seeks engaging and provocative project proposals from independent media producers. We encourage works that address contemporary issues, reflecting the growth and change in our communities

NATIONAL BLACK PROGRAMMING CONSORTIUM
4802 Fifth Avenue
Pittsburgh, PA 15213
(phone) 412-622-6443
(fax) 412-622-1331
Web: nbpcinfo@blackstarcom.org www.blackstarcom.org
Non-profit national media arts organization dedicated to the funding, promotion, presentation and distribution of quality Black film and video projects. Through their annual Request For Proposals (RFP), NBPC seeks contemporary films about the Black experience for the National PBS Schedule.

NATIONAL ENDOWMENT FOR THE ARTS
1100 Pennsylvania Avenue NW
Washington, DC 20506-0001
Phone: 202.682. 5742
Email: webmgr@arts.endow.gov
Web: www.arts.gov
NEH is an independent grant-making agency of the U.S. government, dedicated to enriching American cultural life by promoting knowledge of human history, thought and culture. Priorities include subjects of national significance, projects geared to diversified audiences, collaboration with other cultural organizations and the use of multiple formats or interactive media technology. implementation and production.

NATIONAL ENDOWMENT FOR THE HUMANITIES (NEH)
1100 Pennsylvania Ave, N.W.
Washington, DC 20506
Phone: 1-800-NEH-1121
Fax: 202-606-8400
TDD: 202-606-8282
Email: info@neh.gov
Web: http://www.neh.gov
Offers grants for independent filmmakers and digital media producers whose work addresses significant subjects in the humanities; reaches broad public audiences; grows out of sound scholarship; and uses imaginative, engaging formats.

NATIONAL FOUNDATION FOR JEWISH CULTURE
Fund for Jewish Documentary Filmmaking
330 Seventh Avenue, 21st floor
New York, NY 10001
Phone: 212-629-0500
Fax: 212-629-0508
Email: Grants@JewishCulture.org
Web: http://www.jewishculture.org/film.htm
The Fund is designed to support the creation of original documentary films and videos that promote thoughtful consideration of Jewish history, culture, identity, and contemporary issues among diverse public audiences. Grant size: $20,000 - $30,000

NATIONAL SCIENCE FOUNDATION
4201 Wilson Blvd.
Arlington, VA 22230
Phone: 703.292.5090
Email: info@nsf.gov
Web: www.nsf.gov
Supports media projects designed to deepen the appreciation of science and technology and the understanding of the impact science and technology has on today's society. Projects generally develop materials and programs that reach large audiences and have the potential for significant regional or national impact.

NATIONAL VIDEO RESOURCES
73 Spring Street, Suite 403
New York, NY 10012
Phone: 212.274.8080
Fax: 212.274.8081
Email: nvrinfo@nvr.org www.nvr.org
Web: www.nvr.org/
Assists in increasing the public's awareness of and access to independently produced media & film and video as well as motion media delivered through the new digital technologies. Commissions and publishes research on issues of concern to independent media makers, distributors, educators, activists and individuals.

NATIVE AMERICAN PUBLIC TELECOMMUNICATIONS
1800 N. 33rd St.
Lincoln, NE 68583
Email: native@unl.edu
Website: http://www.nativetelecom.org
Supports program ideas that bring new perspectives on Native American cultures to public television audiences, increasing the quality and quantity of Native American television programming on a national and international scale.

NEW FILMMAKER EQUIPMENT GRANT PROGRAM
Oppenheimer Camera
666 S. Plummer St
Seattle, WA 98134
Phone: 206-467-8666
Fax: 206-467-9165
Email: filmgrant@oppenheimercamera.com

Website: http://oppenheimercamera.com/grant2.html
Supports new filmmakers in producing their first serious film project. The grant awards the use of their Grant Program Arriflex 16SR camera package to senior and graduate thesis students and to independent filmmakers for a scheduled period of time. Proposed projects may be of any non-commercial nature: dramatic, narrative, documentary, experimental, etc.

NEXT WAVE FILMS
Web: www.nextwavefilms.com
Phone: 310.392.1720
Company of the Independent Film Channel, provides finishing funds and serves as a producer's rep helping filmmakers implement festival and press strategies and secure distribution. Has expanded its focus to include documentaries.

NEXTPIX
295 Greenwich St. Ste. 348
New York, NY 10007
Phone: 212.465.3125
Fax: 212.658.9627
Email: info@nextpix.com
Web: www.nextpix.com.
Deadline: September 15 New York city-based production company, is offering post-production grants to first- and second- time filmmakers. The projected budget cannot exceed $250,000.00, and principal photography must have been completed after January 1, 2000. Production must be completed and the project must be in post-production.

OPEN MEADOWS FOUNDATION
PO Box 150-607
Van Brunt Station
Brooklyn, NY 11215-0150
(phone) 718-768-4015
Email: openmeadows@igc.apc.org
Website: www.openmeadows.org
Projects that have limited financial access which reflect the cultural and ethnic diversity of our society and promote the empowerment of women and girls; and projects for social change that have encountered obstacles in their search for funding. Grants: Up to $2,000

PACIFIC ISLANDERS IN COMMUNICATION
1221 Kapi'olani Blvd., #6A-4
Honolulu, HI 96814
(phone) 808-591-0059
(fax) 808-591-1114
Email: info@piccom.org
Website: http://www.piccom.org/
National nonprofit media organization established primarily for the purpose of increasing national public broadcast programming by and about indigenous Pacific Islanders. Sponsors Open Door Completion Fund and Media Fund

PACIFIC PIONEER FUND
PO Box 20504
Stanford, CA 94309
(phone) 650-497-1133
Website: www.pacificpioneerfund.com
CA, WA, OR Documentary Filmmakers. Grant size: $1,000 - $10,000.

PANAVISION'S NEW FILMMAKER PROGRAM
6219 DeSoto Ave.
Woodland Hills, CA 91367-2602
http://www.panavision.com
Submit proposals three months before you intend to shoot. Donates 16mm ADD and 35 mm camera packages to short, non-profit film projects, including graduate student thesis films, of any genre.

PAUL ROBESON FUND FOR INDEPENDENT MEDIA AKA FUNDING EXCHANGE
Ms. Trinh Duong, Program Officer Funding Exchange
666 Broadway, Suite 500
New York, N.Y. 10120
Phone: 212-529-5300
Fax: 212-982-9272
Email: fexexc@aol.com
Web: www.fex.org/robeson
Preproduction funds & distribution funds for projects by organizations & indep artists.. Topics of interest: AIDS and other health issues, racial & gender justice, reproductive rights, homelessness, welfare reform, women, gays, lesbians, disabled persons. Artists from communities of color and people with little recourse to other funding encouraged to apply.

PEW CHARITABLE TRUSTS
2005 Market Street, Suite 1700
Philadelphia, PA 19103-7077
Phone: 215.575.9050
Fax: 215.575.4939
Email: info@pewtrusts.com
Support nonprofit activities in the areas of culture, education, the environment, health and human services, public policy and religion. Makes strategic investments that encourage and support citizen participation in addressing critical issues and effecting social change.

PLAYBOY FOUNDATION
Playboy Foundation
680 North Lake Shore Dr.
Chicago, IL 60611
Phone: 312.751.8000
Web: www.playboy.com/pd-foundation.
Supports media projects that help to foster open communication about and research into human sexuality, reproductive health and rights; protect and foster civil rights and civil liberties in the U.S. for all people, including women, people affected and impacted by HIV/Aids, gays and lesbians, racial minorities, the poor and the disadvantaged; and eliminate censorship and protect freedom of expression. Projects must have nonprofit fiscal sponsorship to be eligible

POTRERO NUEVO FUND PRIZE
1246 Folsom St
San Francisco, CA 94103
Phone: 415-626-5416
Web: http://www.newlangtonarts.org/
Bay Area only. Up to four $12,500 awards for artist's projects on urban and social environmentalism.

PRINCESS GRACE FOUNDATION
150 East 58th Street, 21st Floor
New York, New York 10155
Phone: (212) 317 1470
Fax: (212) 317 1473
Web: http://www.pgfusa.com/index.htmlMs
e-mail: pgfusa@pgfusa.com

Dedicated to identifying and assisting young talent in theater, dance and film through grants in the form of scholarships, apprenticeships and fellowships.

PUFFIN FOUNDATION
20 East Oakdene Avenue
Teaneck, NJ 07666-4198
Phone: 201-836-8923
Fax: 201-836-1734
Email: puffingrant@mindspring.com
Web: www.angelfire.com/nj/PuffinFoundation
Grants that encourage emerging artists whose works, due to their genre and/or social philosophy might have difficulty being aired. Grants: Up to $2,500
REGIONAL ARTS ORGANIZATIONS
http://www.arts.gov/artforms/RAO_SAAs.html#RAOs
Works with the Arts Endowment utilizing funds mandated by the Congress as well as funds from state governments and other sources.

RESIST, INC.
259 Elm Street
Somerville, MA 02144
(phone) 617-623-5110
Email: resistinc@igc.apc.org
Website: http://www.resistinc.org
Distribution costs of film and video linked to social justice organizing.
RETIREMENT RESEARCH FOUNDATION
http://www.rrf.org/welcome.html
Operates a general grants program, two award programs (ENCORE and the Congregation Connection Program) open to Chicago-area nonprofits only, and the National Media Owl Awards, a national film and video competition.

ROBERT FLAHERTY FILM SEMINAR
Web: http://www.flahertyseminar.org
Various educational and grant opportunities to artists in film and video.

ROBERT WOOD JOHNSON FOUNDATION
Web: http://www.rwjf.org/index.jsp
RWJF's mission is to improve the health and health care of all Americans. The Foundation has goals and interest areas related both to health and health care.

We rarely make grants for publications or media projects, except those that grow out of one of our grant programs.

ROY W. DEAN GRANT
From The Heart Productions
1455 Mandalay Beach Road
Oxnard, California 93035-2845; www.fromtheheartproductions.com
Email: CaroleEDean@worldnet.att.net
LA Film and LA Video Grants; NYC Film Grant; Editing Grant; Writer/ Researcher Grant. Multiple grant programs for student filmmakers, independent producers, or independent production companies producing documentaries, shorts, or low budget indies. Looking for film and video projects that are unique and benefit society. New projects, works-in-progress, length is not a consideration.

SCHOTT FOUNDATION
T678 Massachusetts Avenue, Suite 301
Cambridge, Massachusetts 02139
Phone: 617-876-7700
Fax: 617-876-7702
Web: http://www.schottfoundation.org
Focuses on the development of: universal and accessible high quality early care and education excellent public schools in underserved communities gender healthy public schools. The Foundation is always interested in learning about the programs and projects like-minded organizations are doing. Funds research and media campaigns for public awareness.

SCOTTISH SCREEN
Isabella Edgar, Information Manager
Phone: 0141 302 1730
Fax: 0141 302 1778
Web: http://www.scottishscreen.com/
Scottish Screen develops, encourages and promotes every aspect of film, television and new media in Scotland. Working with the Scottish Executive, our mission is to establish Scotland as a major screen production center and project our culture to the world.

SISTER FUND
116 East 16th St., 7th Floor
New York, NY 10003
(phone) 212-260-4446
(fax) (212) 260-4633

Email: sisterfund@aol.com
Support for programming that fosters women's and girls' economic, social, political, and spiritual lives with a primary emphasis on national advocacy and media strategies to heighten public consciousness around issues affecting women and girls.

SOUTHWEST ALTERNATE MEDIA PROJECT (SWAMP)
1519 West Main
Houston, TX 77006
Phone: 713.522.8592
Fax: 713.522.0953
info@swamp.org
Promotes film, video and new media through education, information and presentation activities. Provides a non-profit umbrella for established media artists seeking grants and contributions to develop and produce film and video.

STANDBY PROGRAM
Box 184
NY, NY 10012-0004
Phone: (212) 219-0951
Fax: 212- 219-0563
Provides artists access to quality video postproduction. services at reduced rates. Non-profit media arts organization dedicated to providing artists and independent makers access to broadcast quality video post-production services at extremely discounted rates.

STATE AND JURISDICTIONAL ARTS AGENCIES
http://www.arts.gov/artforms/RAO_SAAs.html
Works with the Arts Endowment utilizing funds mandated by the Congress as well as funds from state governments and other sources.

STATE HUMANITIES COUNCILS
http://www.neh.gov/whoweare/statecouncils.html
56 humanities councils located in U.S. states and territories support local humanities programs and events.

SUNDANCE DOCUMENTARY FUND
8857 West Olympic Blvd.
Beverly Hills, CA 90211
Email: sdf@sundance.org

Web: www.sundance.org
No deadline. Supports international documentary films and videos focused on current and significant issues and movements in contemporary human rights, freedom of expression, social justice, and civil liberties. Development funds up to $15,000 and Production/Post-Production to $50,000, though most will be around $25,000.

TEXAS FILMMAKERS' PRODUCTION FUND
http://www.austinfilm.org/site/PageServer
Phone: 512-322-5192
Web: www.austinfilm.org
The Texas Filmmakers' Production Fund is an annual grant awarded to emerging film and video artists in the state of Texas. Grants: $5,000.

THANKS BE TO GRANDMOTHER WINIFRED FOUNDATION
P. O. Box 1449
Wainscott, NY 11975
Phone: (516) 725-0323
2 deadlines annually (postmarked): March 21 and September 21. Provides funding for women over 54 years of age to create and manifest into reality, ideas and concepts that will improve the lives of women in one or more aspects.

THIRD WORLD NEWSREEL
545 Eighth Avenue, 10th Floor
New York, NY 10018
Phone: 212-947-9277
Fax: 212-594-6417
Web: http://www.twn.org
Committed to the creation and appreciation of independent and social issue media by and about people of color, and the peoples of developing countries around the world.

UNITARIAN UNIVERSALIST FUNDING PROGRAM/FUND FOR A JUST SOCIETY
P.O. Box 40
Boston, MA 02117
(phone) 617-247-6600
(fax) 617-247-1015
Email: uufp@aol.com
Website: http://www.uua.org/uufp/

Funds film/video only if it is an integral part of a strategy of collective action for social change. Grants to $10,000; most in the $5,000 to $7,000 range.

VISUAL STUDIES WORKSHOP MEDIA CENTER
Phone: 716-442-8676
Accepts proposals on an ongoing basis for its media access program. Artists, independent producers, and nonprofits working on noncommercial projects are awarded reduced rates for production and post-production equipment.

WALLACE ALEXANDER GERBODE FOUNDATION
Thomas C. Layton, President,
The Wallace Alexander Gerbode Foundation
470 Columbus Ave., #209
San Francisco, CA 94133-3930
Phone: 415.391.0911
Email: maildesk@gerbode.org
Web: www.fdncenter.org/grantmaker/gerbode/
Applications are accepted on an ongoing basis.   Interested in programs and projects offering potential for significant impact. The primary focus is on the San Francisco Bay Area (counties of Alameda, Contra Costa, Marin, San Francisco and San Mateo) and Hawaii. To qualify for support, an organization must be a tax-exempt public charity, as determined by Internal Revenue Code Section 501(c)(3).

WEBCINEMA
http://www.webcinema.org
A nonprofit organization dedicated to the independent filmmaker using internet new media technologies to finance, create, produce, distribute and market independent film.

WOMEN IN FILM AND TELEVISION
8857 West Olympic Blvd., Suite 201
Beverly Hills, CA 90211
Phone: 310-657-5144
Fax: 310.657.5154
LA: http://wif.org/home/index.html
NY: http://www.nywift.org/Women In Film
Offers various programs

WOMEN IN FILM FOUNDATION

http://www.wifti.org/
Various programs including completion funding and in-kind contributions
to independent producers and nonprofit organizations for documentary,
dramatic, educational, animated and experimental film and videos.

WOMEN IN THE DIRECTOR'S CHAIR
941 W. Lawrence #500
Chicago, IL 60640
Phone: 773-907-0610
Fax 773.907.0381
Email: widc@widc.org
Web: htttp://www.widc.org/
Various Programs

WOMEN MAKE MOVIES
462 Broadway Suite 500
New York, NY 10013
Phone: 212-925-0606
Fax: 212-925-2052
Email: info@wmm.com
Website: http://www.wmm.com/
Major distributor of film and videos by women. Offers fiscal sponsorship
programs, Proposal writing workshops, networking opportunities with other
women media makers, and discounts at labs and equipment facilities.

Top Corporations with a Heart for Documentary & Independent Filmmakers

Dallas

Panavision Dallas
Camera rentals & repairs. Panavision, Arriflex, and Moviecam cameras. 35mm, 16mm,HD Camera equipment, and helicopter mounts. Full lighting packages with supertechnocrane, remote heads, dollies, and jib arms. 8000 Jetstar Drive Irving, Texas 75063 (972) 929-8585 -O (972) 929-8686- fax (800) 260-1846- Toll Free

Los Angeles
Ace Rentals Generators for all of your production needs. Call Gabby at:626-584-1201

Acey Decy Equipment rentals, sales & service for films, TV & events. Grip trucks, Moving lights, special effects. 818-408-4444

Airstar Lighting Balloons Unique balloon lighting for films, TV & events. Call tool free: 1-800-217-9001 for ideas on how to use balloon lighting

Alan Audio Works 562 408-6821 Jeff Alan writes music for all films and donates music to two of our winners per year.

American Cinematheque
Specialty film programming at Hollywood's Historic Egyptian Theater. 323-461-2020

Botas Music Pro! - Bobby Robinson - www.bobbyrobinson.com Composer, song writer, and lyricist.18415 19th St. KPN Lakebay, WA 98349, USA Phone: 253-884-2385 or Toll Free # 877-GO BOTAS; botasmusic@aol.com

Cassius Weathersby Experienced feature and commercial production manager. 310-281-7540

Certified Printers Inc.
Hollywood's one-stop source for printing and copying.
1525 N Cahuenga Blvd
Hollywood, CA 90028
323-465-5411

CFI Film Laboratory 4050 Lankershim Blvd., N. Hollywood, CA 91604

Copywrite Duplication Bob Carboni 323-461-4151 transfer from film or tape to DVD

Coufal-Isley Sound Call Leo 323-871-9288 for your audio equipment rentals

Carole Joyce Photography Stills and head shots. 805-984-5796

Documentary Doctor, Fernanda Rossi. Story Development, Analysis and Editing, Postproduction Supervision and Planning. www.documentarydoctor.com

Edgewise Special discounts on all film, video and data media products. Ask for Hank at (800)824-3130

Eric Galler FMC Corp. Independent filmmaking professionals, superior at the craft of post production supervision. 7095 Hollywood Blvd. Suite #858 323-467-6580

Eric Hamburg Still Photographer www.hamburgfoto.com

Film Arts Foundation San Francisco. Call 415-552-8760 kcs@filmarts.org for editing, fiscal sponsorship(they can be a 501 C3 not for profit sponsor for filmmakers), and other services

Hollywood Production Audio, Ask for Mr. Lawrence Freid 213-250-5550 sound equipment rental

Howard Wexler Director of Photography for feature films, shorts, documentaries, educational, corporate and industrial film and video projects.
961 Vernon Ave. Venice, CA., 90291 310-396-3416

Indiewire For current daily industry news on your computer for free! http://www.indiewire.com, (212) 877-4325

John Gilbert, A.C.E Award winning Editor for docs and films Gilly3000@aol.com

John Lugar Director, Writer, Producer. JLProd@msn.com

Joseph Pier, DGA DP - Camera - live action photographers
www.AVisualGroup.com

Louise Hogarth, IATSE "Dream Out Loud Produtions" Producer &
director of Academy Award winning documentaries. dol@artnet.net

Lightning Dubbs 1/2", 3/4", 1", Beta, Betasp, Beta SX, CDROM, D1,
D2, Digital S., Digital Beta, DVCAM, DVCPRO & DV. 953 N. Highland
Ave. Hollywood, Ca. 90038, (323) 957-9255 1831 Centinela Ave.
Santa Monica, Ca. 90404 (310) 453-3777

Mark Litwak Hollywood's foremost production attorney. 433 N.
Camden Drive, Ste. 1010, Beverly Hills, CA 90210, Phone:(310)859
9595, Fax: (310) 859 0806, atty@marklitwak.com,
www.marklitwak.com

Morrie Warshawski Consultant, facilitator and writer who has spent
over 25 years specializing in the nonprofit arts sector.
www.warshawski.com

Otto Nemenz Corporation Best cinematographic equipment for filming
323-469-2774
Karl Kresser has 16 & 35mm cameras

Party Organizers Specializing in catering of wrap parties, martini
bars, coffee bars and waitstaff. 323-969-0858 , 1340 N. Curson, Suite
#108, Los Angeles, CA 90046

Raleigh Studios A major supplier of stages, lighting, screening rooms,
and equipment for the film industry. 5300 Melrose Ave., Hollywood,
CA 90038 AND 1600 Rosecrans Ave. Manhattan Beach, CA 90266
323.466.3111

REEL EFX Inc. A major supplier of special effects equipment for the
film industry.
5539 Riverton Ave. N. Hollywood, CA 91601 818-762-1710

Sam Dlugach Exposure Pictures Production & Post Avid DV 3.5 and
Final Cut 3.0 Editorial DaVinci Color Correction for Film, HD, SD,
and DV Expert Post-Production Consultation P.O. Box 304 Burbank,
CA 91503 818-563-4124

Smart Girls Productions Marketing services for actors and writers.
Query letter mailings to agents and producers. Cover letters to

agents, casting directors, and managers. 15030 Ventura #914 Sherman Oaks, CA 91403 818-907-6511 smartgirls@smartgirlsprod.com

Solvent Dreams (323) 906-9700Complete post production from DV to HD. Edit suites, editors, motion graphic artists, sound designers, composers, colorists that put their heart into your project. We serve the community of filmmakers

T & T Optical Effects
A top producer of titles and opticals.
818-241-7407

Tiffen Filters 516-273-2500 Carol, cposnack@tiffen.com

TheWWWeb.company Internet promotions, website optimizations, web advertising & more, PO Box 1074, South Lake Tahoe, California 96156, (530) 544-8923, (530) 544-8924 fax Theweb@thewwweb.com

Universal Studios Sound editing & post production services. 818-777-2211. 100 Universal City Plaza, Universal City, Cal. 91608

Video Works -John Rupert- Experienced producer, director, and director of photography. Expert in film and video production. Video Works, 874 Walnut Ave #B, Carpinteria, CA 93013, 805-684-7000, 805-966-7033, vidsonic@silcom.com

Wiseman & Burke, Inc. Business and financial management services to clients including entertainers, health care professionals, and business executives. 818-247-1007. 206 S. Brand Blvd., Glendale, CA. 91204

Write Brothers, Inc. (formerly Screenplay Systems)
The most innovative tools for film, TV & creative writing. Phone: 800-84-STORY Int'l: 818-843-6557 www.screenplay.com

New York

AAA Communications Rental, Sales & Service of Walkie-Talkies, Cell Phones & Pagers. 210 Fairfield Rd, NY, 973-808-8888

Abel Cine Tech, INC. Professional Motion Picture Equipment Rental, Aaton 16mm & 35mm & all related Accessories. 66 Willow Ave. #201 Staten Island, NY 10305 718-273-8108

Analog Digital International: Video tape transfers in all formats, high quality duplication, AVID rentals, on/off line editing.
20 E 49th Street - 2nd Fl New York, NY 10017 212-688-5110

Athamas Studios Digital Compositing, 2d animation, Storyboarding or PriViz, DVD authoring, and DV editing. Rochester, NY 525-249-5127 athamas@mac.com

Botas Music Pro! - Bobby Robinson - www.bobbyrobinson.com Composer, song writer, and lyricist.18415 19th St. KPN Lakebay, WA 98349, USA Phone: 253-884-2385 or Toll Free # 877-GO BOTAS; botasmusic@aol.com

C'est Fou! Special events producers.
307 E. 67th St. #10 New York, N.Y. 10021, 212-288-6085

Cineric Restoration
Digital effects, title design, video to film transfer & more
603 9th Avenue, NYC, NY 10036, 212-586-4822

Documentary Doctor, Fernanda Rossi.
Story Development, Analysis and Editing, Postproduction Supervision and Planning. www.documentarydoctor.com

Eastman Kodak Company Sales of motion picture film and print stocks. 360 West 31st. St., Suite 710, New York City, New York 10001, 212-631-3400

Edgewise Ask for Hank 800 8243130, he has special discounts for all filmmakers and gifts for the winners of the grant.

Film/Video Arts: The largest non-profit media arts center in the NY region, provides independent filmmakers with low-cost training, equipment rental, & editing services. 817 Broadway, 2nd Fl. New York, NY 10003, 212-673-9361

Magno Sound & Video: Complete Audio, Video & Film post production facility. 729 Seventh Avenue New York, NY 10019, 212-302-2505

Metro Access DSL Digital editing for entire film. Studio time and editing for a 5 min trailer 204 East 23rd St., NYC NY 10010, Mr. Jim Chladek

Sensory Lab Visual Communications design firm specializing in print, interactive, motion graphics, 3d modeling and animation. 416-883-0562   Design@sensorylab.com

Sound Dimensions Complete Audio post-production services. Recording, sound mixing, sound design & transfers. 321 West 44th Street New York, NY 10036 212-757-5147

Tape House, NY Full Duplication Services, Specializing in Digital Formats, Fiber Optic National & International Connections. 216 East 45th Street New York, NY 10017, 212-557-4949

TheWWWeb.company Internet promotions, website optimizations, web advertising & more, PO Box 1074, South Lake Tahoe, California 96156, (530) 544-8923, (530) 544-8924 fax Theweb@thewwweb.com

Tiffen Filters 516-273-2500 Carol, cposnack@tiffen.com

Unilux INC. Provides High Speed Stroboscopic Lighting Equipment for Film & Video Productions. 59 North 5th Saddle Brook, NJ 07663, 201-712-1266

Write Brothers, Inc. (formerly Screenplay Systems)
The most innovative tools for film, TV & creative writing. Phone: 800-84-STORY Int'l: 818-843-6557 www.screenplay.com

New Zealand

Avalanche Lighting
Fully equipped lighting truck & gaffer. Specialists in commercials & feature films. NZ, Phone: 09 360 8110 mobile: 025 434 224

Bytesize
Paul Davidson, Director / Editor, documentary, corporate, audio-visual production. PO Box 38, Renwick, Marlborough. Phone 03 572 9683 Fax 03 572 9722 Email paul@bytesize.co.nz

Data Book
New Zealand's Film, Video and Television Production Industries Directory. www.databook.co.nz,   PO Box 5544, Wellesley Street, Auckland, NZ, Phone: 0-9-630 8940

David Editing
David Tokios, Avid Management LTD, Level 1 283 Parnell Road,
Parnell, Auckland, NZ
Phone: (64 9) 377 7095

Digital Post
3D computer animation, VFX, graphics, film post, I. T. K. Millennium
& Cintel Ursa Gold telecines, & more. 7 Owens Road, Epsom,
Auckland, Phone: +(64 9) 630 1770

The Film Unit Limited
Laboratory, film & sound post production, film to tape transfer and
theatres. 1 Fairway Drive Lower Hutt, Wellington, NZ Phone: 04 920
5500

Kodak New Zealand
Film stock, sound & still stock suppliers.
70 Stanley St., Parnell, Auckland, NZ, Phone: 09 302 8665

Panavision
Camera rentals & repairs. Lighting & still equipment sales & studio.
The Production Village, 27 Napier St., Freemans Bay, Auckland, NZ,
Phone: 09 360 8750, Phone: 09 360 8760

Tait Mobile Radio
Two Way Radio Short and long term hire, 761 Great South Road ,
Penrose, Auckland, New Zealand Phone: 09 579 0000
www.taitmobile.co.nz, Rentals@taitmobile.co.nz

TheWWWeb.company Internet promotions, website optimizations,
web advertising & more, PO Box 1074, South Lake Tahoe, California
96156, (530) 544-8923, (530) 544-8924 fax Theweb@thewwweb.com

FOOTNOTES

i The Foundation Center. (2002, June). Foundation Center Releases Update on Arts Funding Trends. Retrieved January 14,2003 from: http://fdncenter.org/media/news/pr_0205a.html

ii The Business Committee for the Arts. (2002). 2001 National Survey of Business Support to the Arts. Retrieved February 3, 2003 from: http://www.bcainc.org/programs.asp?pg=2

iii The Business Committee for the Arts. (2002). Poll Indicates Business Support to the Arts Will Remain Stable in 2003. Retrieved February 3, 2003 from: http://www.bcainc.org/programs.asp?pg=2

iv Alison Landsberg, "Prosthetic Memory: The Logic and Politics of Memory in Modern American Culture" (Ph.D. dissertation, University of Chicago, 1996).

v The United Arts Funds Report Fiscal Year 2001. Published by Americans for the Arts. September 2002. Washington, DC.

Share The Art of Funding

It's easy to order more copies of
The Art of Funding Your Film: Alternative Financing
Concepts

1. Fax Orders to 1-805-984-5796
2. Mail the order form below to: Dean Publishing, C/O Carole Dean, 1455 Mandalay Beach Road, Oxnard, CA 93035, USA
3. Call toll free 1-866-689-5150 (24-hours a day, 7 days a week) *Please speak clearly and specify all of the information requested on the order form below.*
4. E-mail: caroleedean@att.net

Please send me the following items. I understand that I may return them if I am not satisfied in 60 days for a full refund.

Description	Price	Quantity		Total
Trade Paperback	$28.85	X	= $	_____
Videocassette	$ *	X	= $	_____
		Sub Total	= $	_____
	California Shipments add 7.5% Sales Tax		= $	_____

Choose Shipping and handling options:

U.S. Ground, rate add $2.00	= $	_____
U.S. Air add $4.00 for the first item	= $	_____
+ $2.00 for each additional item	= $	_____
International Rate add $9.00 for the first item	= $	_____
+ $5.00 for each additional item	= $	_____
TOTAL = $		_____

Your Name: _____

Address _____

City _____ *State/Province* _____

Zip/Postal Code _____

Country _____

Home Ph ( ) _____ *Work Ph ( )* _____

Check _____ *Visa* ___ *Mastercard* _____ *Optima* _____ *Amex* _____

Credit Card # _____ *Exp. Date* _____

Cardholder's Name _____

(as it appears on card)

Signature _____

I want more FREE information on: Consultations □ *Other books* □
Video Seminars □   *Upcoming Seminars* □   *CD/DVD* □

* Please check our web site at www.fromtheheartproductions.com
for information about videocassettes and other products